STORIES FOR BOYS WHO DARE TO BE DIFFERENT 2

Running Press Kids
Hachette Book Group
1290 Avenue of the Americas, New York, NY 10104
www.runningpress.com/rpkids
@RP_Kids

Printed in Germany

Originally published in Great Britain in March 2019 by Quercus Editions Ltd, a Hachette UK company

First U.S. Edition: October 2020

Published by Running Press Kids, an imprint of Perseus Books, LLC, a subsidiary of Hachette Book Group, Inc. The Running Press Kids name and logo is a trademark of the Hachette Book Group.

The Hachette Speakers Bureau provides a wide range of authors for speaking events. To find out more, go to www.hachettespeakersbureau.com or call (866) 376-6591.

The publisher is not responsible for websites (or their content) that are not owned by the publisher.

Illustrations by Quinton Winter.

Cover design by Arnauld.

Interior design by Sarah Green.

Library of Congress Control Number: 2020934922

ISBNs: 978-0-7624-7215-4 (hardcover), 978-0-7624-7214-7 (ebook)

MOHN

10   9   8   7   6   5   4   3   2   1

STORIES FOR BOYS WHO DARE TO BE DIFFERENT

EVEN MORE TRUE TALES OF AMAZING
BOYS WHO CHANGED THE WORLD

Ben Brooks

ILLUSTRATED BY QUINTON WINTER

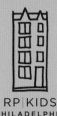

RP | KIDS
PHILADELPHIA

CONTENTS

CARLOS ACOSTA

(BORN 1973)

Carlos grew up in a poor neighborhood in Cuba. He was kicked out of school when he was young, and his dad ended up in prison. Carlos was sent to the National Ballet School of Cuba simply because it was a place that could afford to feed him.

But his natural talent soon became apparent.

In 1990, Carlos won the Prix de Lausanne, a competition that pits hundreds of dancers from across the world against each other.

Carlos then traveled to Russia and became the first foreign person to become a guest artist for the Bolshoi Ballet. At twenty-five, he became the first black person to become a principal dancer at the Royal Ballet in the United Kingdom, as well as the first black person to play Romeo in a ballet.

"Nobody who looks like me has ever played the roles I dance," said Carlos. "When I first appeared in *Swan Lake* at the Metropolitan Museum of Art in New York, the auditorium was packed with black people."

He blew spectators away with his speed, precision, grace, and power. His otherworldly, flowing, electrified way of moving brought new life to many old ballets.

But ballet is famously tough on the body. Joints creak, feet bleed, and blisters form and burst. At forty-two, Carlos embarked on a farewell tour to mark his retirement from ballet. Five thousand people a night would turn up to cheer and cry as the dancer who'd lit up their lives whirled across the stage for the final time. After his last performance, the audience hurled roses onto the stage and gave him a standing ovation that lasted an entire twenty minutes.

Carlos is now creating an academy in Cuba where people can study dance for free, hoping to nurture the beloved dancers of the future.

NOUSHAD AFRIDI & KHITTABSHAH SHINWARI

In 2002, a British reporter named Amardeep Bassey traveled to Afghanistan to chronicle the impact that the American invasion was having on its people. It was a dangerous place and, for safety, he hired two local guides, Noushad and Khittabshah.

Both Noushad and Khittabshah belonged to Pashtun tribes who dwell in the Khyber Pass, a dangerous, mountainous route that is the main connection between Afghanistan and Pakistan. Together they helped Amardeep successfully cross from Pakistan to Afghanistan. In the capital city of Kabul, the reporter interviewed ordinary people about how the war had affected their daily lives. Then he headed back into Pakistan with Noushad and Khittabshah.

They were stopped at the border. Amardeep was told he didn't have the correct visa to pass through.

"You two may go," the border guard told the Pashtun tribesmen. "But we are taking him."

The guards were convinced that Amardeep was an Indian spy. They hauled him off to jail, where he was locked in a small cell filled with robbers, murderers, and terrorists. Coming from the West meant he would have very likely been a huge target for violence inside the prison. However, he was not alone. Noushad and Khittabshah had volunteered to be arrested alongside him. They were not going to abandon a man they'd promised to protect.

"Without them, I would have crumbled," said Amardeep.

The two men looked after him for twenty-eight days. When Amardeep was finally released, they were made to stay inside the jail until he'd left Pakistan.

The three of them kept in touch. Some years later, Amardeep returned to Pakistan to thank the men who went through prison to help a stranger from a distant land.

IBRAHIM AL HUSSEIN

(BORN 1988)

Ibrahim grew up with thirteen siblings in Deir ez-Zor in Syria. They would spend their days playing basketball, practicing Judo, and swimming in the blue waters of the Euphrates River. Then civil war broke out.

One day, Ibrahim was in the street when rockets crashed down around him. He threw himself into the nearest building for cover. That was when he started hearing cries for help. His friend had been hurt and was lying in the open.

Sprinting out to help him, Ibrahim was struck by a rocket.

He managed to haul himself to safety, but the damage to his leg was irreparable. It had to be amputated. Medical services and supplies were so limited that Ibrahim woke up twice during the harrowing operation and was sent home the next day without any pain relief.

Seeking better medical care, Ibrahim traveled to Turkey and made the dangerous crossing to Greece on a rubber dingy. He was granted asylum and settled in Athens. Initially, Ibrahim used a wheelchair for transport but was eventually fitted for a prosthetic leg. He used it as a chance to get back into swimming.

Two years later, Ibrahim competed in the Paralympics in Brazil, as part of the Independent Paralympic Athletes Team, a group made of refugees and asylum seekers. He was also chosen by Greece to carry their Olympic torch. Proudly, Ibrahim raised the lit beacon as he walked through a refugee camp in the center of Athens.

"I am carrying the flame for myself," Ibrahim said. "But also for Syrians, for refugees everywhere."

There are now an estimated sixty-five million displaced people around the world. Ibrahim hopes he can act as proof they can rebuild their lives.

BISI ALIMI

(BORN 1975)

It is unthinkably dangerous to be gay in Nigeria. You can be sent to prison for years or even be sentenced to death. As a result, almost no Nigerians are openly gay. In 2004, Bisi became the first person ever to come out on Nigerian television.

Bisi was an actor on a popular show, and various people who knew about his sexuality had been threatening to use that information against him. Bisi decided to take control before the declaration took him by surprise.

It cost him everything.

His character was immediately killed off, the live element of the show he'd come out on was canceled, no one would give him any other work, and he was subjected to years of cruel discrimination. Leaving the house became a huge risk. Bisi found ways to become involved with outreach work, trying to educate gay men about the dangers of HIV. But Nigeria was no longer safe for him.

One night, a group of men broke into Bisi's house. They tortured him and his boyfriend. The only way the couple could survive was to flee the country.

Bisi was given asylum in Britain in 2009 and has been living there since. He's earned a university degree in global governance, has worked for various charities, and has now set up his own organization: the Bisi Alimi Foundation. They aim to tell the stories of lesbian, gay, bisexual and transgender (LGBT) people in Nigeria, put pressure on employers and politicians to open their hearts to them, and draw the world's attention to how painful life is for gay people there. Bisi hasn't given up hope of making a difference.

"I am a prisoner of hope," he says. "I believe that we do move as human beings and we do change. I strongly believe that Nigeria is going to change."

AMROU AL-KADHI

(BORN 1990)

Amrou prefers not to be called "he" or "him." At first, it can be slightly confusing for those who aren't used to it, but avoiding these pronouns can help people who don't feel comfortable being gender-defined.

Amrou prefers "them" and "their." "It feels like a warm bath," they say. "It makes me feel like I'm being heard and that someone sees me, not for being a 'man,' but for being Amrou."

And Amrou often didn't feel seen. Growing up, their parents would tell them that their walk wasn't like a proper man's and that their voice wasn't how a man's should be. Amrou's parents' religion made them fear their child's differences. They banned Amrou from anything remotely bright or exciting and became furious if they caught them looking at anything related to being gay.

Amrou found escape in two different places. The first was on the stage, where they could bury themselves in a role and become someone else. The second was with their face pressed up to an aquarium, where they could glimpse another world of fantastical, beautiful creatures who seemed somehow both alien and wise.

Amrou worked as hard as possible to get a scholarship which meant they could leave home and finally have some freedom. That was when they started performing in drag, under the name of Glamrou and also as part of a troupe called Denim. Drag meant dressing up in flowing wigs, extravagant makeup, and flamboyant outfits. It also meant being able to take control of how you're seen and break free from traditional ideas of gender. Soon, Amrou was throwing drag balls for hundreds of university students.

After university, Amrou would go on to perform sell-out shows, star in and write films and TV shows, and publish a book about their life, titled *Unicorn*.

Sometimes, while performing in drag, Amrou thinks of themselves as an aquarium. Though they're separated from the rest of the room, they offer a window into a sparkling new world, one which Amrou hopes can offer courage to those who haven't yet discovered who they are.

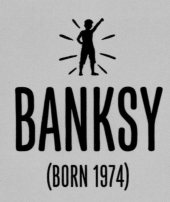

BANKSY

(BORN 1974)

Some people think he's a famous musician. Some people think he's a group of seven artists working together. Most people think he's a boy from a small town near Bristol. But no one knows for sure.

All we really know is that Banksy's artworks began appearing on the walls of buildings in Bristol during the 1990s. They were surprising, strange images that were anti-war and anti-establishment. In one, a young girl watched her heart-shaped balloon drift away. In another, a rioter hurled a bouquet of flowers.

At London Zoo, Banksy found a way to climb into the penguin enclosure and spray-painted "We're Bored of Fish" on the rocks inside it. On the wall separating Israel and Palestine, he painted a beautiful view of a tropical island and two kids playing with buckets and shovels.

In the dead of night and in total secrecy, Banksy roamed through cities, leaving behind beautiful murals and unexpected images.

After a huge painting of a man hanging from a window appeared on a doctor's office in Bristol, a vote was held about whether to keep it: 97 percent of residents voted for it to stay.

His work went from being seen as vandalism to being seen as valuable art. People were buying prints of his work for thousands of dollars. Banksy used this to help others. When a school in Bristol named one of its houses after him, administrators woke up to find an original Banksy on the school's wall. When a youth club in Bristol was on the brink of closing down, Banksy sprayed a piece onto it and they sold it for $450,000, more than enough to keep them going for years.

Banksy never thought much of the traditional art world. When one of his paintings sold for $1.1 million at an auction, a secret shredder built into the frame destroyed it in front of everyone, leaving the buyer with a few scraps of paper.

Through an illegal form of art, Banksy unexpectedly gave back to communities, brightened people's lives, and brought excitement into streets around the world.

JAMES MATTHEW BARRIE

(1860–1937)

You may have heard the story of the boy who never grew up and the adventures he had in Neverland, alongside Wendy, Tinkerbell, and the Lost Boys. The story of *Peter Pan* was first written by a man named James Matthew Barrie.

James grew up in Scotland. He had nine siblings, though two died before he was born.

When James was just six, disaster struck again: his older brother died in an ice-skating accident. It devastated their mother, as the brother had been her favorite, but through a shared love of stories, she and James drew closer and closer.

At school, James spent most of his time reading, playing pirates, and putting on plays with the drama club he'd formed with friends. He knew he wanted to be an author and went to college to study literature. After that, James wrote books for adults. They tended to be funny and strange, but none would quite capture the imagination of the world like the magical children's story he went on to write.

The first time the character of Peter Pan appeared was in a book written by James called *The Little White Bird*, but it was on the stage when he really came alive. The play was called *Peter Pan, or The Boy Who Never Grew Up*, and it was a hit. James had used various elements of his own life to weave the tale: the Saint Bernard dog he shared with his wife, the games of pirates he'd played at school, and the memory of his older brother, who'd never had a chance to grow up.

The play was a huge and instant success. James turned the story into a novel, which has since been made into countless films and theatre productions.

When he died, James left the copyright earnings from *Peter Pan* to Great Ormond Street Children's Hospital. The boy who never grew up is, to this day, helping children who one day will.

CHESTER BENNINGTON

(1976–2017)

Chester had a difficult childhood: he was bullied at school for being small and looking different and was abused for several years. His parents divorced when he was eleven. He frequently ran away from home. The only way he could truly escape was through painting pictures, writing poems, and penning songs.

Chester eventually dropped out of school and worked at a Burger King. Sometimes he played with bands, though they never had any success. Disheartened, Chester thought about quitting music entirely.

Then he was asked to audition for a new band that was being put together. Chester missed his own birthday party to record a demo. The other members were blown away by his vocals, which would soar from quiet whispers to furious screams of rage.

He joined a rapper, Mike Shinoda, as well as several other musicians, to form the band Linkin Park. Their first album, *Hybrid Theory*, came out in 2000 and became the bestselling rock album of the twenty-first century.

The band combined metal, rap, and electronic music to create an unheard-of sound that blasted from the bedrooms of teenagers everywhere.

In Linkin Park songs, Chester sang openly about his struggles with mental health, which millions related to. When he sang about the whirlwind in his head, the pain of living in his own skin, and the search for somewhere to belong, people felt like they were listening to someone who understood them.

Linkin Park sold more than 100 million albums. They've since been cited as an influence by everyone from bands like Imagine Dragons to rappers like Stormzy.

Unfortunately, in 2017, Chester took his own life. The mental health issues he'd suffered since childhood became overwhelming and he felt unable to access the help that was available. Fans, family, and celebrities gathered together at his funeral to celebrate Chester's life and listen to the songs he'd given to the world.

TIM BERNERS-LEE

(BORN 1955)

Tim's parents worked on the first computer ever available to buy in stores: a five-ton machine that would fill a whole room. He grew up entranced by talk of mathematics and complex code. A love of toy trains also gave him his first glimpse into the world of electronics, and Tim was soon constructing his own gadgets.

He kept working on his creations throughout college. Using an old calculator, broken television sets, and a car battery, Tim built his very own computer terminal. After using it to hack into the physics mainframe, the university banned him from accessing the system.

Tim traveled to Switzerland to work as a computer programmer. What frustrated him most about his work was how much data there was and how difficult it was to share. He came up with a way of computers interacting with each other to make the process easier. When Tim released the source code for free, his creation rapidly took on a life of its own.

The internet was born.

It has gone on to shape societies, businesses, and governments, infiltrating every aspect of our lives and putting everyone on Earth only a click away.

Tim worries about the state of the internet today. It was meant to be a network that would bring everyone together, give everyone equal access to opportunities and education, and allow people to work together to build a better future. Instead, he is concerned it has been taken over by large corporations who use the data of its users for profit and power.

He's urging people to fight back and reclaim the internet as theirs. He has created a number of online organizations meant to give people understanding of the issues related to them.

Tim himself never made any money from the internet. Getting rich was never what it was about. He cares more about helping people.

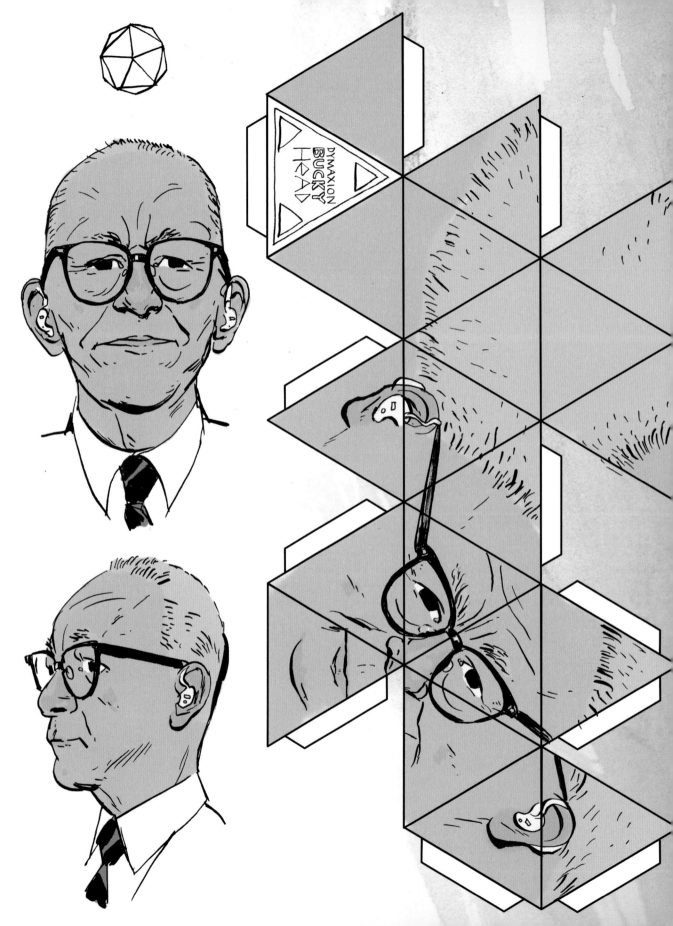

DYMAXION
BUCKY
HEAD

RICHARD BUCKMINSTER FULLER

(1895–1983)

Richard struggled at school, particularly with mathematics. It just didn't quite make sense to him that a dot on a blackboard would correspond to a mathematical point.

He preferred working with his hands. Often, Richard would spend hours scouring the woods for lost or discarded pieces of metal. He used scavenged parts to construct his very first invention: a kind of mechanical system for rowing a boat.

Richard was kicked out of school twice. Life after that didn't get any easier. He lost a child, lost his job, and found himself living in poverty.

One day, distraught and hopeless, Richard went down to the banks of Lake Michigan and considered throwing himself in. That was when he heard a voice that told him he was part of the universe and had a duty to remain alive and do his best to help others.

He went on to create a number of inventions. The most well-known was the geodesic dome, a kind of structure built of tiny triangles that would prove to be incredibly strong. He also invented a new type of car, called Dymaxion, which had three wheels and could seat eleven people. Neither invention caught on, though both looked like things that had come from the future.

The domes finally came to be used for other purposes; they were adopted by the military and used in weather stations, homes, and storage depots.

When a molecule was discovered that almost identically resembled the geodesic dome, scientists named it Buckminsterfullerene.

Richard believed that everyone is born a genius, and it is only the process of living that "de-geniuses" them. The trick is to pick a path you're passionate about and stick to it at any cost.

*Turn to the last page of the book to make your own geodesic dome

ROBERTO BURLE MARX

(1909–1994)

As a teenager, Roberto moved from Brazil to Germany to study painting in college. There, he found himself spending more and more time wandering through the grand Botanical Garden of Berlin.

Strangely, it was only in these German gardens that Roberto first truly appreciated the beauty of Brazilian orchids, palms, and waterlilies; plants rarely celebrated back home.

Once he returned to Rio de Janeiro in 1930, Roberto turned his home into a rambling center for tropical plants. He went on long expeditions through the rainforest in search of rare specimens and ended up discovering several unknown ones along the way.

With these newfound plants, Roberto began creating exquisite gardens throughout his city. He drew inspiration from modern art, Brazilian folk art, and nature itself. With unique water features, swathes of tropical vegetation, and whirling mosaics, Roberto went on to produce some of the most exciting and unique gardens ever seen. Some of his most well-known include the Copacabana Beach promenade, the UNESCO building gardens in Paris, and the lush Flamengo Park, built on an old landfill site in Brazil.

"Unlike any other art form," said Roberto, "the garden is designed for the future, for future generations."

He thought the same of the rain forest, too, and was one of the first prominent Brazilians to speak out against the destruction of the Amazon rain forest. At a time when so much money was flowing into the country through logging and other environmentally damaging activities, it was a bold stance. The companies responsible for deforestation were powerful and ruthless.

Roberto died in 1994. He left behind more than two thousand beautiful gardens and discovered almost fifty new species of exotic plants.

LOYLE CARNER

(BORN 1994)

Loyle was diagnosed with attention deficit hyperactivity disorder (ADHD) at an early age. He found that cooking was a great way to help him fully relax. He also found an outlet in writing, though his dyslexia meant teachers told him to pursue something else. He didn't listen. He wasn't about to stop expressing himself through words.

By the age of eighteen, he performed his first official rap gig under the name of Loyle Carner. A year later, he released his own CD, *A Little Late*. It was seven months after his stepfather had died and Loyle had turned his pain, rage, and grief into a set of songs that would resonate with fans everywhere.

While performing a huge concert at Glastonbury Festival, Loyle brought his mother up on stage to dance. His family has always been his biggest influence. Both of his parents appear in recordings on his album and sometimes, while he raps, he clutches a jersey that once belonged to his dad. He said that by the end of the Glastonbury show, the audience was full of men crying, and that he felt it was heartwarming and vital, because

sometimes we all need that kind of release.

In October 2017, Loyle was in the news for throwing a man out of his performance after he heard him shouting something rude at a woman. Some people said it was to be expected at a hip-hop concert. Loyle put his foot down.

"Hip-hop," said Loyle, "comes from poetry and jazz and blues and pain and people expressing how they feel. Not from treating women with disrespect."

Loyle's still touring the world, as well as opening a culinary school for kids with ADHD. He hopes he can help them find a creative outlet for their feelings, the same way he has.

ROBERT CHAN

With turquoise waters, deep lagoons, lush forest, and pristine beaches, the islands that make up Palawan are some of the most beautiful in the world. But every day, they face all kinds of threats, which Robert Chan spends his life fighting.

Illegal loggers chop down trees, illegal miners search for gold, and illegal poachers snatch pangolins and mynah birds from their dens. Robert Chan leads the resistance against these activities with a group called the Palawan NGO Network Inc. (PNNI). They are a team of sixteen civilians trying their best to preserve their home.

The members spend days on long, treacherous missions through jungles and mountains in search of illegal activity. If they come across any, they order the men responsible down onto the ground and take away their tools. None of the PNNI carry any weapons. They use only their knowledge of the area, firm commands, and the ability to make citizen's arrests.

It is a dangerous task. Since 2001, twelve members of the PNNI have been killed by those seeking to turn Palawan's beauty into money.

"We had to do enforcement work because the government wasn't doing it," Robert said. "We can't stand watching our resources being destroyed in front of our faces."

When Robert opposed the expansion of mines on Palawan, the governor of the islands threatened to personally fight him. It can all get so serious and stressful that sometimes he likes to unwind by singing karaoke.

Robert's office is decorated with confiscated chainsaws, dynamite, axes, and guns. They serve as a warning of the kind of brutal damage people are capable of inflicting on the environment and a reminder of everything the PNNI are up against. In fact, so many chainsaws have been collected that a permanent Christmas tree has been built from them, and that tree stands outside the Palawan Environmental Enforcement Museum.

THE CHERNOBYL DIVERS:
ALEXEI ANANENKO, BORIS BARANOV & VALERI BEZPALOV

This is the story of three Russian men who sacrificed their lives to save millions more. Though their names may have been largely forgotten, the impact of their actions is still felt around the world.

On April 26, 1986, the reactors of the Chernobyl Nuclear Power Plant blew up, releasing a toxic cloud of radioactive material that spread over Europe. Almost 400,000 people had to leave their homes.

Ten days after the first explosions, it was discovered that the plant's cooling system had gone wrong, leaving a pool of water below the extremely radioactive reactor. Scientists realized that if nothing was done, a lava-like substance would melt through the final safeguards, dropping the reactor into the pool and triggering a series of explosions. They would destroy entire cities and leave Europe uninhabitable.

A team of three employees stepped up to help. Alexei Ananenko, Valeri Bezpalov, and Boris Baranov volunteered to swim into the power plant and drain the water through the release valves. Alexei was the only person who knew where the valves

were, Valeri was a soldier and an engineer from the plant, and Boris was a worker who offered to go along and hold the lamp. They all agreed to go despite knowing the levels of radiation were so high they would all probably die.

They put on scuba gear and went in. Over the next few days, they drained almost five million liters of water from the plant, averting a crisis of unthinkable proportions.

Since that day in 1986, the Chernobyl disaster has claimed thousands of lives. Without the bravery and selflessness of those three divers, the figure would have stood in the millions.

JIMMY CHOO

(BORN 1948)

Jimmy's father was a shoemaker who ran his business
from the family home. Jimmy was eleven when
he first learned how to put together a shoe. His dad hadn't
forced him to; he just wanted Jimmy to have something
to fall back on if life didn't turn out how he wanted it to.
But Jimmy was hooked.

After a visit to family in London, Jimmy learned about Cordwainers Technical College and decided to go there to study shoemaking. He had to work cleaning restaurants to earn enough to get by.

Once he'd completed his course, Jimmy rented a run-down old hospital building that he used as a base for designing, making, and selling his shoes. It was a makeshift operation, but one that was fueled by Jimmy's spirit and devotion. Word began to spread about the man from Malaysia who painstakingly made beautiful shoes by hand. One day, *Vogue* ran a huge spread about his work. The next day, Princess Diana called and asked if he'd consider creating a pair of shoes for her.

Jimmy phoned his father to tell him the good news.

"You're not a famous designer," his father said. "Why does she want you?"

Jimmy pondered this and decided it was probably because hardly anyone has the skill to make shoes by hand anymore. Thousands of people can draw designs, but only a very few can actually use their own two hands to make those designs a reality.

The shoe company Jimmy Choo still produces some of the most colorful, extravagant, and sought-after shoes in the world.

Now Jimmy is working to build a shoemaking institute in Malaysia so that young people there can have the same opportunity to hone their craft as he did. He wants to promote education, innovation, and the kind of traditional craftsmanship his father taught him.

JOHN COOPER CLARKE

(BORN 1949)

John caught tuberculosis as a boy, which left him weak and prone to catching illnesses. While other kids were outside playing, he'd have to stay indoors, alone with his thoughts.

He first fell in love with poetry thanks to an English teacher at school who would recite from the nineteenth-century Romantic poets to the class and encourage them to learn the verses by heart. The teacher explained that once you've learned a poem by heart, it's something you'll always carry with you.

John knew he wanted to become a poet, but he wasn't sure how to go about it. Where were the poets? he wanted to know. He couldn't see any in Manchester.

Instead of going to bookshops or libraries, John would tour with punk bands and rock musicians. Before they played sets, he'd get up on stage with nothing but a microphone and belt out his strange, dark, funny poems to the cheers and whoops of amazed crowds.

The audiences recognized his rebellious spirit and welcomed him as one of their own.

He wrote about everything from marrying a space alien to holidays in Majorca, and from the poor streets of his town to losing a Kung Fu fight. One of his poems, "I Wanna Be Yours," is frequently read at weddings and was turned into a hit song by the Arctic Monkeys. Another poem, "Evidently Chickentown," was read at the closing scene of one of the biggest American television dramas of all time.

John is in his seventies now. He still has huge spiky hair, wears tight jeans with dark sunglasses, and sells out whole theatres to people who want to spend an evening listening to him read his poems.

CYRUS THE GREAT

(600 BC–530 BC)

When Astyages, King of Media, had a dream that one of his grandsons would go on to overthrow him as king, he ordered them all to be killed, including Cyrus. Fortunately, a servant felt pity for Cyrus, spared him, and raised him in secret.

Cyrus did grow up to take the throne from his grandfather. With courage and intelligence, he led the Persians in a series of campaigns that would establish the largest empire in the world.

One of his biggest victories was gaining control of the Babylonian kingdom. In 587 BC, the Babylonians had invaded Jerusalem and thrown Jews out of their homes, forcing them to live in exile. Once the Jewish people heard that Cyrus was moving in, they returned to welcome him as a liberator and help him defeat the Babylonians. Cyrus then permitted all of the displaced Jewish people to return to their homes in Jerusalem and practice their beliefs without fear of persecution.

Unlike the conquerors and rulers that had come before him, Cyrus was kind, generous, and tolerant to those who found themselves under his rule.

He did not force them to abandon their religions or customs and didn't try to destroy their societies and rebuild them to suit himself. Instead, Cyrus aimed to achieve peace among men.

In 1879, a piece of baked clay was found in the ruins of ancient Babylon. It became known as the Cyrus Cylinder and showed the very first declaration of human rights in existence. Cyrus declared that he would never allow slavery, never allow theft of land or property, give everyone the freedom to practice whatever religion they wished to follow, and never allow one group of people to oppress another. He'd known from a young age how it felt to be unfairly persecuted and had made certain that those living under him didn't feel the same way. Two thousand, five hundred years ago, Cyrus had been fighting for freedoms that many are still denied today.

THE 14TH DALAI LAMA

(BORN 1935)

Dalai Lama is the name given to the spiritual leader of the Tibetan people. He acts as a symbol of hope, peace, and goodness for the Buddhists of Tibet and beyond. Every time one Dalai Lama dies, search teams are sent out to find his reincarnation to become his successor, as Buddhists believe we live in cycles of birth, death, and then rebirth.

When communist China invaded Tibet in 1949, over a sixth of its population was killed and 6,000 monasteries destroyed. It is still ruled fiercely by the Chinese, who have stripped its people of their freedoms, destroyed 80 percent of its forest for their own profit, and dumped their nuclear waste across the country. Because of this, a large number of Tibetan people live in exile.

One of these exiles is the 14th Dalai Lama.

He was discovered as a two-year-old boy whose parents were horse traders living in a remote mountain town. He eventually traveled on an epic journey across Tibet (with a caravan of Muslim traders for his protection). The Buddhists were forced to pay huge amounts to the Chinese government to guarantee his safety. Once he reached Lhasa, the capital of Tibet, he studied until the age of fifteen, when he became the 14th Dalai Lama.

In 1959, some Tibetan groups tried to fight back against the Chinese. China invaded to crush the rebellion and, fearing for his life, the Dalai Lama fled.

He now lives in India, where he spreads ideas of peace, love, and understanding. Despite the suffering inflicted on Tibet by China, the Dalai Lama has always maintained that they should fight back only with nonviolent resistance. Hundreds of thousands of Tibetans would gladly have taken up arms to fight back against their Chinese oppressors had their leader called for it, but he never once has. For this, the 14th Dalai Lama was awarded the Nobel Peace Prize in 1989.

"The true hero," he says, "is the one who conquers his own anger and hatred."

MAHMOUD DARWISH

(1941–2008)

At the age of seven, Mahmoud and his family were forced out of their home in Galilee as the Israeli Army occupied Palestine. Later, they secretly returned, only to find their village destroyed. The military had taken power.

Mahmoud wanted to help maintain an identity for the people of Palestine and vowed to keep his homeland alive through poetry.

At nineteen, he published his first collection, *Wingless Birds*. He also left what had now become part of Israel to study abroad in Russia and Egypt. When he tried to return, he found he was banned from the country he had once called home for becoming involved with a group that supported freedom for Palestinians. He was eventually allowed to move back to one certain area but never felt safe or at peace.

Meanwhile, his poetry was being translated around the world and winning multiple awards.

Despite his popularity, Mahmoud tended to prefer being alone and only had a small group of friends. It did nothing to lessen his popularity. Whole stadiums sold out to hear Mahmoud read. He was soon known as the national poet of Palestine.

Sometimes he would get frustrated that people imbued his poems with so much political meaning. When he wrote about his mother, people would assume she was a metaphor for Palestine, his home country. Actually, most of the time, he was just writing about his mother.

However they're interpreted, Mahmoud's poems keep on resonating today. As Palestinians continue to struggle against Israeli occupation, many still hold Mahmoud's poetry close to their hearts. It serves as a reminder of home, of hope, and of humanity.

He once wrote:

From my brow bursts the sword of light

And from my hand springs the river's water . . .

The people's hearts are my identity.

Go, take my passport away.

SERGEI DIAGHILEV

(1872–1929)

Sergei's mother died when he was young, leaving him to be raised by his stepmother, Elena, and his father, Pavel. The entire family went bankrupt when he turned eighteen, and Sergei had to use the small inheritance he'd received from his mother to keep them afloat.

He went to law school at first but dropped out to focus on his passion: music. This path quickly came to an end, as well, when Sergei was told by one of the world's most famous composers that he had absolutely no talent.

In Paris, Sergei assembled the most exciting choreographers, writers, artists, and designers to create a ballet company unlike anything anyone had ever seen. He called it the Ballets Russes.

They had wild, unrestrained new choreography. Their costumes were flamboyant and fabulous. And the sets were designed by the leading modern artists of the time. They got rid of old ideas about women dancing delicately and men hovering in the background and turned old stories on their heads.

The Ballets Russes took the world by storm, even though they never had any regular funding and Sergei was often on the brink of bankruptcy.

Sergei was also openly gay and had a habit of falling in love with his dancers and becoming inconsolable when they left him.

Despite all this, the Ballets Russes were in demand all across Europe. Much of the music Sergei commissioned for his productions has gone on to become iconic. "Rite of Spring" by Stravinsky, for example, has been recorded at least once almost every year since it was first written and used in films like Disney's *Fantasia* and *The Lost City of Z*.

During a visit with the king of Spain, Sergei told the monarch, "Your Majesty, I am like you. I do no work, I do nothing, but I am indispensable."

Sergei discovered he had a talent for making things come together, and he used it to change the world of performance forever.

HENRY DUNANT

(1828–1910)

Henry was hopeless at school. After being kicked out of college, he took on an apprenticeship and became a banker.

One summer, Henry was traveling through Italy for work when he stumbled across the aftermath of the Battle of Solferino. He was horrified by what he saw. Thousands and thousands of men lay dead and dying across the battlefield, with no one to offer them help. Henry encouraged local villagers to aid the wounded without discrimination. It was a new idea at the time. Generally, people would only give help to those who had fought for their own side.

And so the Red Cross was created.

It would go on to become a worldwide movement with around seventeen million volunteers. They saved lives in the First and Second World Wars, in refugee crises, in natural disasters, and even just in helping people who feel alone in their community. The Red Cross offers aid to everybody.

But Henry didn't think his work was done. Many atrocities were still committed during wartimes, and he wanted to lay down a set of rules that would prevent them from happening in the future.

Henry traveled across the globe once more, asking governments to send some of their personnel to a meeting. Over thirty-nine representatives turned up, and they all went on to sign a series of treaties known as the Geneva Conventions. A vital set of rules still used today, the Geneva Conventions set out how people ought to be treated during wartime. They said that any member of the military who had surrendered or been captured could not be treated badly, hurt, denied medical care, executed without a trial, or dealt with differently based on religion, race, gender, wealth, or anything else.

Despite the impact he had on the world, Henry ran out of money and was left alone in a hospice due to illness. A few years before his death, a teacher discovered Henry and brought him to the attention of the world. Henry was awarded the very first Nobel Peace Prize, and he gave all his prize money to charities.

OSCAR EKPONIMO

(BORN 1986)

After his dad got sick, Oscar and his siblings had to get by on just one main meal every two days. He was living in Nigeria, a country where seventeen million people feel severe hunger every day.

His mother worked as a nurse, but the pay was so little she couldn't afford much. Most days, Oscar would stare into their empty kitchen cabinets, wishing they would fill with food.

Fortunately, Oscar's dad got better and was able to go back to work and earn money to feed the family. Oscar would never forget the experience and vowed to help as many people as he could who found themselves in a similar situation.

With a group of friends, he started a group called Blue Valentine, which gave out free meals to kids living on the street. This, though, was only a small-scale solution to a problem that was affecting 223 million people in sub-Saharan Africa.

Oscar wanted to think bigger.

He'd become an adept software developer by then and decided to turn his technological expertise to the problem at hand. The result was an app called Chowberry.

Every day, supermarkets and shops throw out tons of food simply because it's past the dates printed on the packets. What Chowberry aimed to do was link the stores who were about to throw out perfectly good food with charities that could swiftly distribute the produce to those who needed it most. It would give the shops a solution to the problem of what to do with the excess, as well as keep thousands of people fed for far less money.

Roughly one-third of all the food made to be eaten by humans ends up getting lost or wasted. Hopefully, with the help of Chowberry, some of that can be redirected to the families who have no idea how many days it will be until their next meal.

EDWARD ENNINFUL

(BORN 1972)

Edward's mother was a seamstress, and he'd spend his days dashing between her legs with ribbons of fabric or sketching his own designs. He never thought fashion could be a career, though. Instead, his parents encouraged him to become a lawyer.

One day, when Edward was seventeen, he was on a train when he noticed a man was staring at him. It made Edward nervous.

"I'm the stylist for a magazine," the man said. "How would you like to model for us?" Edward said he'd have to ask his mom.

A few weeks later, he was posing in his first photo shoot and knew that he'd found the world he belonged in. He wasn't going to be a lawyer. It upset his father, but Edward's mother knew that he'd been in love with fashion ever since he was tiny and that it was a positive force in his life.

Edward was always asking if there was work he could do. He became an assistant to the stylist, then a stylist in his own right and was soon hired by *i-D* magazine as its fashion director, becoming the youngest one in Britain at the age of just eighteen.

He learned about how to tell stories through clothes and how to present street fashion. He learned how to style covers and write features. Most nights, he was up until 4 a.m. getting the magazine ready.

At twenty-one, Edward came out as gay. His mother wasn't at all surprised, but it worried his father, who wasn't quite sure what it meant and was concerned for Edward and his career. He needn't have been.

In 102 years of publishing, Edward became the first ever male editor of British *Vogue*.

He has made sure to champion the rights of everyone, including transgender people and gay men and women. "Diversity is not just about being black or white," he says. "I'm always worried about leaving anyone out."

Now, Edward's father reads every issue of *Vogue* the day it comes out. He knows his son is doing what he was born to do.

RUBÉN FIGUEROA

Every year, thousands of Central Americans go missing in Mexico while trying to make the difficult and dangerous journey into the United States. A man named Rubén has made it his mission to track down those who have disappeared.

Often, those attempting the journey can become victims of criminal gangs, find themselves abandoned in the desert by those they paid to help them, and can even be brutally mistreated by the authorities. Rubén estimates that more than seventy thousand Central American people have gone missing in this way.

Rubén himself was once a migrant, making three attempts to cross the border before finally making it across and settling in North Carolina. He worked as a builder for years until a trip back to Mexico made him realize the pain and danger people were enduring to try and make it to a place where they hoped life might be better.

And things were getting tougher for migrants.

After plans were put in place to cut down migration from Central America to the United States, many migrants chose to start taking less obvious routes. Instead of traditional ways through boarding houses in towns and cities, they might travel on the roof of an extremely risky train known as the Death Train or pick paths through dense forest filled with violent smugglers.

Rubén's organization is called the Mesoamerican Migrant Movement. They use computers, documents, and public pressure to fight for migrants' rights and track down those who are missing. They also organize groups of mothers and fathers from El Salvador, Honduras, Guatemala, and Nicaragua into bands who together travel along the migratory routes through Mexico, in a desperate bid to find new information about their loved ones.

In 2013, Rubén received death threats from the gangs he was drawing attention to. The government failed to offer him any protection. It didn't matter. He wasn't going to let intimidation come between him and his goal of reuniting families.

Since the organization was founded, they've reunited 269 missing people with their families.

SIMON FITZMAURICE

(1973–2017)

Simon was a young director with a glittering career ahead of him. He'd made two short films and received rapturous praise. Then, shortly after the premiere of his second film, he was diagnosed with ALS, a condition that would get worse and worse, leading his body to become weaker and weaker. He was thirty-four years old and doctors told him he had only four years to live.

The news didn't slow Simon down. He was determined that, while he was alive, he was going to carry on breathing life into the stories that took shape in his head.

As his illness progressed, Simon couldn't swallow, speak, or breathe without help from machines. He could, however, use eye-tracking technology to write a memoir and direct a feature film.

The book was titled *It's Not Yet Dark*, while the film was titled *My Name is Emily*.

The first told of Simon's struggle with his illness and his desire to make the most of his remaining time on this planet, regardless of what doctors said or how much his body refused to cooperate. The second was the story of a girl who is bounced between foster homes and subjected to callous treatment, only to fall in love and reconcile with her father. Both were powerful accounts of lives lived to the fullest against all expectations.

"For me," Simon wrote, "it is not about how long you live, but about how you live."

After suffering from the disease for nearly a decade, Simon passed away at the age of forty-three. He lives on in his wife, three loving children, and thousands of fans.

In remembering him, his sister, Kate, said, "He always found the beauty, the vulnerable beauty in a person."

AARON FOTHERINGHAM

(BORN 1991)

Aaron was born with a condition called spina bifida, which meant his spine hadn't developed properly. He was adopted at the age of two months. His adoptive parents were worried he would struggle with his physical condition.

Very quickly, they realized that wasn't an obstacle for him. They'd catch Aaron sliding headfirst down staircases or bounding down hallways on his crutches, wearing a cape. He even wrote a comic about a superhero named Crutch Boy.

As it became clear that Aaron's arms and legs wouldn't be able to support his body, he switched from using crutches to manipulating a wheelchair.

Aaron had an older brother who would spend long afternoons at a skate park, and Aaron would often go along to watch. After a while, some of the skaters suggested he try dropping in to a ramp—in his wheelchair.

Aaron fell out and hit the ground. But it was so exhilarating that he got back up and did it again. And again. And again.

The wheelchair wasn't built to be thrashed around a skate park. It broke almost immediately. His friends raised enough money to have a custom

sports wheelchair built that could withstand all the spins, grinds, and aerials Aaron had planned to do.

On July 13, 2006, Aaron landed the world's first ever wheelchair backflip. Video footage of the achievement went viral.

Four years later, he successfully completed the first ever double backflip.

Aaron's proved that his wheelchair doesn't get in the way of life; it helps him do things he'd never otherwise have dreamed of. He says he's not "in" a wheelchair, but "on" it. The same way a surfer's on a surfboard or a skater's on a skateboard.

Aaron's flipped off fifty-foot mega ramps and launched himself across huge gaps. He's also turned his passion into a sport: WCMX, or wheelchair motocross, which continues to transform the lives of young people everywhere by showing them what they can do rather than pointing out what they can't.

MAMOUDOU GASSAMA

(BORN 1996)

Violence, food shortages, and political instability mean that life for a lot of people in Mali is unbelievably dangerous. Many try to leave by whichever means they can.

In 2017, Mamoudou managed to get out. He reached France after being beaten and arrested on his way through Burkina Faso, Niger, and Libya, then he'd made a long and treacherous journey across the Mediterranean toward Europe. He arrived in Paris as an immigrant without any papers, which meant he couldn't get a job, a house, or a bank account, and he risked being sent back to his country if caught.

One day, while walking up from the Gare du Nord in Paris, Mamoudou came upon a four-year-old boy dangling from the railings of a balcony. The boy's parents had left him home alone while they'd gone shopping, and he'd fallen over the balcony while playing but had managed to hang onto its railings, though he was clearly having trouble holding on. The drop below him was terrifyingly deep. Adults on nearby balconies were desperately trying to reach out to him, but he was too far away from them. Bystanders were screaming. No one knew what to do.

Mamoudou barely paused for thought.

He ran forward and began hauling himself up the balconies toward the young boy. Through courage, fitness, and sheer determination, Mamoudou managed to reach the child and save his life.

As a result of his actions, Mamoudou was granted legal citizenship by the president of France and the mayor of Paris went on to call him "Spiderman."

Mamoudou is now working as a volunteer firefighter in Paris.

As heartwarming as his story is, many people think it shouldn't take climbing a building and rescuing a child to be given what everyone deserves: a safe place to call home.

JEAN GENET

(1910–1986)

Jean Genet was put up for adoption when he was seven months old. One of his foster parents reported that he kept sneaking out at night while wearing makeup. He was soon kicked out and then put in prison for being homeless.

Three years later, he was released and joined the French Legion, only to be dismissed for being gay. Jean roamed around Europe over the next few years, falling in and out of love, stealing to survive, writing poetry, and sleeping on the streets. He passed through Poland, Czechoslovakia, Spain, Italy, Austria, and Belgium dressed in rags and suffering from tremendous hunger.

When he finally got back to Paris, he was arrested for being a vagrant and a homosexual. In prison, Jean and the other prisoners were given pieces of brown paper they were supposed to make into bags. Jean used them to write his first novel, *Our Lady of the Flowers*. When one guard discovered this, he had the papers burned. Jean wrote the whole thing out again. Once he was released, he paid to have the novel printed himself.

The novel was a dark and poetic tale of a drag queen trapped in a prison.

It celebrated the kind of people who were rarely ever celebrated: the poor, gays, and criminals. It caught the attention of all kinds of people and went on to be hugely influential to many writers who would follow.

In 1949, Jean was hauled in front of a court and threatened with life in prison for having so many previous convictions. Three world-famous artists—Sartre, Cocteau and Picasso—went directly to the French president and asked for Jean to be released. "He is the only true genius in France," declared Jean-Paul Sartre, who was himself French.

It worked. Jean was discharged.

In his later years, Jean worked with the Black Panthers in America, who were fighting back against police violence inflicted on the black community, visited Palestinian refugee camps, and campaigned tirelessly for the poor.

JOHN GURDON

(BORN 1933)

"I believe he has ideas about becoming a scientist," read John's school report. "This is quite ridiculous." John was ranked last out of 250 boys in his school at biology and in the bottom group for every other subject. Regardless of how interested he was in science, it seemed doomed to remain a hobby.

After receiving such a dismal report, John decided it would be best to study something else, so he chose to pursue Classics at Oxford University. Luckily, something got mixed up in the admissions office, and he was allowed to embark on a Zoology course instead.

A few years later, John performed a groundbreaking procedure. He plucked a cell from the intestine of a frog, isolated its genes, and put them into an egg cell. The result was a clone of the original frog.

It was a monumental achievement and went against everything scientists believed at the time. The results were so unexpected that it would be ten years before everyone accepted them. Once they finally did, the process was used in the cloning of Dolly the sheep, as well as the use of stem cells to replace damaged or sick tissues in living human bodies.

Years later, when John got a call saying that he'd won the biggest prize in science, he thought it was a friend putting on a funny voice and pulling a prank. It wasn't. For his discovery that cells can be reprogrammed, John had won the Nobel Prize.

John is proof that what happens in school doesn't necessarily determine the course your life will follow. You never know where you'll end up, and John has hung his old school report above his desk to remind him of that.

YANG HAK-SEON

(BORN 1992)

When Yang's father suffered a serious injury and could no longer work as a builder, his family moved out of the city and into the countryside. They had to assemble their own shelter out of sheets of plastic and scraps of wood, which was uncomfortable and unsafe, especially during the heavy rain season. It became Yang's dream to one day build his parents a house that would feel like a home.

Yang started training in gymnastics when he was nine. He became interested while watching his brother. In competitions as a teenager, it was clear that he had talent.

At the 2011 World Championships, Yang wowed everyone by performing a previously unseen vault. It consisted of a front handspring and triple-twisting somersault. At the time, the move was described as the most difficult in the world. They named it "The Yang," as he was the only person in the world capable of executing it.

A year later, at the London Olympics, Yang became the first ever South Korean to win a gold in Olympic gymnastics.

After his success, the story of Yang's family's financial situation spread. People were shocked. Even Yang's own coach hadn't known that he'd been living in such poverty. In response, the chairman of a huge company donated almost half a million dollars so that Yang could focus on his sport and not worry about money. Then the head of a construction group offered to build a house for Yang and his family. Finally, the owner of the factory producing Yang's favorite kind of instant noodles offered his entire family free noodles for the rest of their lives.

"I actually cannot believe what's happening right now," said Yang, who can finally give his family the home they deserve.

MAGNUS HIRSCHFELD

(1868–1935)

While Magnus was studying at medical school, a gay man who'd been kept locked up for thirty years was paraded naked in front of the students. Even though it was 1888 and homosexuality was illegal in Germany, the cruelty of the act shocked him to the core.

What shocked him even more than the way the man was being treated was that none of the other students seemed to care.

Later, when Magnus had become a doctor, he was leaving his office one evening when he found a distressed soldier struggling with his own homosexuality and waiting to speak to him. Magnus asked the soldier to come back in the morning. But that night, the soldier killed himself.

It made Magnus determined to overturn Paragraph 175, the piece of German law that made being gay illegal.

Magnus managed to take his argument to the government for discussion, but it was shot down. He decided to take a different tactic, choosing to take the chief of police on a tour of gay bars and clubs through Berlin. The commissioner was surprised to find gay people kind, witty, funny, and stylish, rather than the degenerate animals he'd been led to believe they were. Magnus hoped it would lead to him enforcing anti-gay laws less severely.

In the Institute for Sexual Research that he founded, Magnus saw thousands of gay and transgender patients who were hoping to glean a better understanding of their own sexuality. His prescription was to encourage them to be themselves and embrace who they were.

When the Nazis came to power, they destroyed the institute, burned its books, and used its patient lists to round up homosexuals and take them to concentration camps. Magnus fled to France, where he died not long after.

It would take over a hundred years before science and society would catch up with Magnus's revolutionary work. Thanks to his efforts in fighting for the rights of sexual minorities, he will not be forgotten.

SHERIF HOSNY & TAREK HOSNY

Scientists have shown that just being able to see plants, flowers, or trees can relax us, make us happier, and help us become healthier. For two brothers, Sherif and Tarek, growing up in hot, dry Cairo meant they rarely saw much greenery.

During a trip to Louisiana, they first witnessed hydroponic farming. Instead of relying on soil, hydroponics is a way of growing plants using only a small amount of water with nutrients dissolved into it. The technique makes agriculture in dry climates much easier.

Back home in Cairo, the brothers set up an organization called Schaduf that could harness what they'd learned and use it to help their community. They wanted to build tiny hydroponic farms on rooftops so poorer families could use them as a source of extra food or income. First, they worked hard to create the perfect model; then they began to roll it out.

Schaduf would give families loans to set up the farms. If they managed to sell their produce, the loans could be paid back within six months and they'd own their own fully functional rooftop farm.

The organization also created sprawling walls of living vegetation inside offices and apartment blocks, which helps lift the spirits of those who spend so much time inside them.

And the gardens help the environment, as well as the people who live among them. Temperatures in cities can be up to three degrees warmer than outside of them, contributing majorly to global warming. By filling rooftops with greenery, the air around them becomes cooler, shade is provided, and less energy is needed to regulate the temperature inside the buildings below. The plants also create oxygen, helping provide cleaner air among the polluted environment of the inner city.

"We haven't covered the whole of Cairo in green," said Sherif. "But I feel that can happen."

They haven't stopped innovating. The brothers are constantly working on new ideas and projects, always looking for ways to bring more light, life, and nature into downtown Cairo.

WITI IHIMAERA

(BORN 1944)

Witi spent the first years of his life traveling from farm to farm across the north of New Zealand so that his parents could earn money shearing sheep. They settled down when he got older, and Witi was sent to school.

That was when he got his first taste of literature. It amazed him that he could sit down with pages of words and be transported into another time and place. One of his favorite books, *The Good Master*, told the story of a girl living in rural Hungary in the 1930s.

As he got older, his parents went to meet his headmaster, wanting to know if they should pull their son out of school.

"Will he ever become something?" his parents asked.

The headmaster told them he wouldn't. They said it would be better if they took him home and put him to work on the land. Witi's father decided to give him one more chance. That term, Witi wrote his first story. It was enough to convince them he deserved to stay.

He went on to struggle in college and got kicked out. So he returned to his hometown and worked at the local paper. His main task was calling the police station, the hospital, and the airport for stories. He started writing in earnest, too, about native New Zealanders finding their feet in the world.

His breakout novel was titled *The Whale Rider*. It told of a young Māori girl called Kahu, driven to become the chief of her tribe, even after she'd been told that it was a job that only men could do. The book was turned into a film that was successful around the world.

Witi wants to transport readers into the world of New Zealand and its native people, the same way that he was once transported into 1930s Hungary. He continues to fight for the rights of the Māori, as well as recording their triumphs and tribulations in his novels.

Many people consider Witi the first Māori ever to publish a book. As Kahu says in *The Whale Rider*, "I know that our people will keep going forward, all together, with all our strength."

THE JAMAICAN BOBSLED TEAM

When Devon Harris first saw a bobsled in September 1987, he thought to himself, "No one could ever get me to go on one of those. That's crazy." Dudley Stokes, Michael White, and Freddy Powell had never seen one before either. Four months later, all of them would go on to compete in the 1988 Winter Olympics as Jamaica's first ever bobsled team.

The idea was born when two American brothers living in Jamaica witnessed a push cart derby. Contestants would climb inside the carts they usually used as market stalls, and barrel around tricky, winding courses. The two businessmen thought the sport looked remarkably similar to bobsledding and decided to create a Jamaican team.

First, they asked Jamaican athletes, who all said no. A team was recruited from volunteers and members of the army. Devon, Dudley, Michael, and Freddy trained in Austria and miraculously managed to qualify for the Olympic Games. They were all incredibly nervous. They were doing something no one from their country had ever attempted before.

The world watched as a team of four men from a country that had never seen snow entered their first Winter Olympics.

In the two-man bobsled event, they didn't win, but they did manage to beat ten other teams. They'd come so far

that they weren't ready to give up. The men hurriedly raised money by selling t-shirts and bought a four-man bobsled from the Canadian team. They entered that race, too, despite never having tried it before.

Forty thousand turned up to watch the Jamaican team, all of them shouting "Go, Jamaica!" Despite not even coming near to winning a medal, the spirit of the team had captured people's attention everywhere.

They were flying down the track until they hit a wall and crashed. That wasn't going to stop them from finishing! They picked up the bobsled and carried it to the end of the race, with the crowd going wild with applause.

On the journey home, the team worried that their country would be embarrassed that they'd crashed. They weren't. In fact, the Jamaican government put the faces of Devon, Michael, Dudley, and Freddy onto stamps.

AKRIT JASWAL

(BORN 1993)

One day, in India, a young girl suffered an accident that left her hand severely burned. Over the following five years, her fingers became fused together. Her parents didn't know what to do; they lived in the middle of the countryside and had no money. The only hope they had was a seven-year-old boy named Akrit who lived in a nearby village.

People said Akrit was a genius. They said he'd been speaking from the age of one and reading Shakespeare plays and medical textbooks from the age of five. Rumor had it that he'd spent most of his childhood observing surgeons in the local hospital.

So the parents took their little girl to see Akrit. Though the prospect of accidentally hurting the girl was terrifying, there was no other option. As young as he was, Akrit successfully performed surgery on the girl, separating her fingers and saving the use of her hand. Videos of the operation spread across the internet.

Akrit was admitted to medical school when he was twelve. He quickly turned his attention to finding a cure for cancer.

Some people are concerned that having so much attention heaped on a young person can be damaging.

Akrit's talent hasn't come without a cost. After years spent struggling for his son to get recognition and opportunities, Akrit's father became exhausted and ended up leaving the family. Having such a precocious child can put a great deal of pressure on parents. What's the best way to help them flourish? Send them to university, where they'll be years younger than everyone else? Or keep them in regular school, where they're likely to be bored and unchallenged? Being so different can make it hard to find a place to fit in.

But Akrit finally has. He's in his mid-twenties now and studying bioengineering in the city of Kanpur. He's still aiming to find a cure for cancer, which he thinks might be possible using something called oral gene therapy. He is not going to let go of the dream he's had since boyhood.

CARL JUNG

(1875–1961)

Carl was a quiet child who spent a lot of time on his own. He was happiest sitting alone for hours, lost in his own thoughts or solemnly studying.

Life was difficult. Carl's mother suffered from depression and bizarre night-time hallucinations, while Carl himself became convinced that he was two people at the same time.

One day, a classmate shoved Carl to the ground. After that, he fainted at the thought of going to school and soon stopped going at all.

As he grew older, Carl became fascinated with why he behaved the way he did and what made other people act the way they did. What had caused his mother's depression? What had made him think he was two people? Carl looked for answers in dreams, in the folklores of ancient civilizations, and in the depths of his own mind.

He was soon traveling the world gathering research and giving lectures about his ideas. He believed that people fell into two broad groups: either loud and sociable, or shy and happier alone. He called the first type of people extroverts and the second type of people introverts, although he knew that almost everyone was a combination of both.

Carl became one of the most famous psychologists of his time and developed his own theory: analytical psychology. This theory claimed that the way to happiness lies in trying to discover what exactly is unique about you. The more you learn about yourself, the more you understand yourself and the happier you become.

Carl's theories have changed the way we look at ourselves and each other. He played a crucial role in the ongoing quest to help people around the world lead fuller, happier lives.

RICHARD KEARTON
(1862-1928)
& CHERRY KEARTON
(1871–1940)

Richard Kearton was born in 1862, nine years before his brother, Cherry. They both loved being in nature. Richard even fell out of a tree when he was nine while trying to glimpse a bird's nest and walked with a limp thereafter.

When they were grown-ups, the brothers took on jobs for a publisher that involved putting together books of nature photographs. At the time, most wildlife photography meant posing stuffed animals out in nature and taking pictures of them. The cameras were too slow for live ones.

But the Kearton brothers were determined to change things. They wanted to show people the true joy and energy of the animal kingdom.

In April 1892, they took the first ever photograph of a bird's nest filled with eggs. They worked from a ladder tied precariously high onto a tree. They would rappel hundreds of feet down jagged rock faces.

When it came to photographing the actual birds, though, Richard and Cherry found the creatures would all rush away from the loud, slow cameras. To get around this, they built dens out of mud, dens out of stone, and dens made to look like haystacks or piles of turf. The brothers would disguise themselves as tree trunks, as bushes, and even hide themselves inside the bodies of dead cows. For hours and days, they would tramp through the dark, lie soaking wet in gullies, and sleep under the stars, just to get a single photo.

They also fought for the protection of animals. At a time when most safaris meant long trips shooting many animals, the brothers tried to convince people to shoot photos of the magnificent beasts instead.

CRAIG KIELBURGER

(BORN 1982)

At the age of twelve, Craig read an article in his local newspaper in Canada about another twelve-year-old boy called Iqbal Masih, who had been killed on the other side of the planet. Iqbal had been enslaved and made to work in a dangerous factory since the age of four. Once he'd escaped, he'd begun campaigning for the freedom of other child slaves and was shot for having done so.

The story spurred Craig on to research child labor. He was horrified by his findings. With some other kids in his class, he founded a group called Free the Children. The idea of the group was that children could help children without needing the influence of adults.

Their first course of action was to collect three thousand signatures calling for the release of a children's rights activist who had been illegally locked up. Later that year, Craig traveled through India, Pakistan, Nepal, Thailand, and Bangladesh to meet child laborers, human rights activists, and even the president of Canada, who was in the area negotiating trade deals at the time.

By the time he returned home, he had become international news. He was interviewed on various TV channels, gave speeches at schools and colleges, and raised thousands of dollars.

Craig is now in his mid-thirties. The charity is still going.

Free the Children has built over 650 schools in 21 countries, sent over 200,000 healthcare packages abroad, donated millions of dollars of medical aid, and provided clean drinking water for almost a million people. They work closely with schools in both developed and less-developed countries to educate and inspire students.

Donations have come from over a million children in forty-five countries. With Free the Children, they've learned that, regardless of age, they have the power to stand up and make positive changes in a dangerous world.

REUBEN KOROMA & GRACE AMPOMAH:
SIERRA LEONE'S REFUGEE ALL STARS

Reuben Koroma and Grace Ampomah were born in Sierra Leone, a country that has long been torn apart by brutal conflict. As violent attacks take place, ordinary people are forced out of their homes, ending up crossing borders into neighboring countries and living in refugee camps.

After they were married, Reuben and Grace Koroma fled Freetown, the capital of Sierra Leone, in 1997. They made their way into Guinea and settled at a camp called Kalia. It wasn't long before they'd met up with some people they knew from back in Freetown. With two old electric guitars donated by a charity, Reuben and his friends formed the Refugee All Stars.

Their music was bright, upbeat, and likely to get people up and dancing, though the lyrics told of the struggles of being a refugee and of having to leave home.

The band took their music from camp to camp, spreading joy. As they went, a film crew recorded a documentary that would go on to introduce the world to the Refugee All Stars.

"One day you are suffering in this world," said Reuben. "And the next day you are healing other people's pain through music."

Once the war was over, they returned to Freetown, to continue making music. They released an album of recordings called *Living Like a Refugee* that had all been recorded live around the campfires of the Guinea refugee camps. The album was an international success.

The band is still touring, recording, and spreading their message around the world, using their music to draw attention to the plight of displaced people everywhere. Most of the money they make is sent home to help their families and villages.

SAMAN KUNAN
(1980–2018)

In July 2018, a soccer team of young boys went adventuring with their coach in the vast and ancient Tham Luang Cave. They were planning to find a comfortable spot, sit down, and have a birthday party.

But it was monsoon season and, as the boys went deeper into the cave, a relentless downpour began. The cave flooded, and they were forced to seek out a high ledge where they could stay out of the water. Their coach quickly realized that none of the boys could swim.

They were trapped.

As water levels rose and heavy currents swirled, the world watched on, wondering how, when, and if the boys could be rescued. Time was crucial. At any moment, the water levels might rise to the level of the boys' hideout and the available oxygen would run out.

A rescue mission was launched that would go on to involve over ten thousand people. Saman was one of those who rushed to the site immediately, keen to see how he could help. As a retired member of Thailand's elite Navy SEAL (Sea, Air, and Land) force, he had the experience. And he would need it. The complicated nature of the cave structure meant that one diving trip, to the boys and back, would take eleven hours.

The boys were eventually all rescued, eighteen days after first getting stuck in the cave. Saman, however, wasn't so lucky. While diving through the passages to deliver air tanks to the boys, he ran out of air for himself, fell unconscious and could not be resuscitated.

A friend of Saman's recalled that once he said, "We never know when we could die. We can't control that so we need to cherish every day."

His funeral was put on by the king of Thailand and a statue of Saman will soon stand at the entrance to the cave, a reminder of the bravery and selflessness he displayed in ensuring those boys made it out of the Tham Luang Cave alive.

ZACHARIAS KUNUK

(BORN 1957)

Igloolik is a small Inuit village in Nunavut, Northern Canada. It is the home of Zacharias, who was born in a nearby settlement in a house built of dirt and grass.

The people of Igloolik had been offered a connection to national television twice. Both times, they had refused, thinking that by inviting it in, they would end up losing their own culture.

But Zacharias was always mesmerized by moving pictures. He would carve animals out of soapstone and sell them for enough money to buy film tickets. On a trip to an art gallery in Montreal, he bought his own video camera and took it back to Igloolik. Zacharias wanted to make a record of his culture. He wanted to capture the traditional *hukki* dance, the vibrant murals, the dogsleds, and the walrus hunts.

In 2001, Zacharias wrote and directed *Atanarjuat: The Fast Runner*, the first film ever to be written and acted entirely in his native language of Inuktitut. It was a reworking of an Inuit legend that told of a man forced to flee his village after a bitter dispute. The tale is filled with romance, violence, and revenge. It was a story Zacharias had first heard from his mother, and one of the countless pieces of tradition he feared were being lost, as foreign religions, schools, and television replaced four thousand years of spoken history.

The film was a worldwide hit.

"This movie doesn't just transport you to another world," wrote one reviewer. "It creates its own sense of time and space."

It made millions of dollars, was voted the best Canadian film ever made, and, more importantly, preserved an aspect of Inuit culture for generations to come.

JEONG KWANG-IL

(BORN 1963)

From their first days at school, all North Koreans are taught that their leader, Kim Jong-un, is a divine and perfect being, that their country is the greatest country on Earth, and that all other countries are their sworn enemies.

In reality, North Korea is extremely poor, cruel to its people, and intolerant of anyone speaking out against it. Owning anything foreign can get you into serious trouble, as can communicating with the outside world.

Jeong was a trader who had been conversing with South Koreans in order to make deals. Often, when he was talking to traders, they'd arrange to get together and secretly watch American films. He said that through films like *Titanic*, he could feel "the limits of human love and what love is all about. Because in North Korea, you don't die for love. You die for the dear leader."

When it was discovered that he had been interacting with South Koreans, Jeong was sent to a camp for those considered to be a threat to the state. In the prison, he was brutally tortured for months. For days on end, his hands were cuffed high up behind his back, at a height that meant he couldn't stand, sit, or sleep. The pain was so intense

that Jeong confessed to being a spy, just to make it end.

He was sent to a forced labor camp in the mountains. In these places, hundreds of thousands of North Koreans are made to do back-breaking labor. They are barely fed and many die from hunger.

Jeong was freed years later, when it was decided there was no case against him. He fled the country.

Jeong now works to set other North Koreans free. He knows that even if he can't do it physically, at least he can set their minds free from the lies they've been fed since childhood. To do this, he fills memory sticks with films, television shows, and books and smuggles them into North Korea via balloons, people, and even remote-controlled helicopters. These, he thinks, will help open people's eyes to the cruelty of the regime that oppresses them and offer hope.

DASHRATH MANJHI

(1934–2007)

It is sometimes said that certain people would move mountains to help others. Dashrath actually did.

Born to a poor family of laborers in Bihar, India, Dashrath grew up making money by chopping down trees. He left home to work in a coalmine and eventually returned to his village to marry the woman he loved, Faguni.

One day, while Dashrath was working in the fields, a pregnant Faguni left home to bring him lunch and water. As she was crossing the mountain, she slipped, fell, and seriously injured herself.

There was no chance to get her to a hospital quickly. The village was cut off from important services by the mountain. It was a journey of over fifty miles (eighty kilometers) to the hospital. By the time Dashrath reached it, his wife had passed away.

He became determined that nothing like that would ever happen again. Dashrath sold his family's goats, bought a hammer and chisel, and set to work carving a path through the mountain. He created his own technique to break his way through the rocks, which involved making a wood fire on top of them, waiting for the rocks to crack slightly, and then pouring water into the cracks to deepen them. Finally, he would hammer the split rocks to pieces.

After many years, Dashrath was still a long way from completing the path when the village was hit by a drought and most people left. His father encouraged him to move with the rest of the family to a city where they could earn money. Dashrath refused. He continued working at his mountain pass, surviving on only dirty water and leaves.

Dashrath worked at the path all day, every day, for twenty-two years.

The road was completed in 1982. It was 360 feet long and helped to connect villagers to vital services, allowing small cars to pass through and shrinking the distance from fifty miles to just two. When he died, Dashrath was given a state funeral and several films have since been made about his life. The path he created is now called the Dashrath Manjhi Road.

RICKY MARTIN

(BORN 1971)

Ricky was performing from a young age. First, he starred in commercials for food, drinks, and toothpaste. Then, at the age of twelve, he joined a boy band called Menudo. His divorced parents fought against each other for control of Ricky.

The band was hugely successful and the pressure of being a member was immense. They flew around the world on tours, were chased by screaming fans, and had their pictures plastered on the bedroom walls of young people all around South America.

As well as having to perform constantly and cope with being caught between his parents, Ricky had to struggle with realizing he was gay. He knew he was drawn to boys, but he also knew that the Catholic religion he'd been brought up with viewed this as a sin. Just wanting to be accepted, he tried his best to bury his feelings.

Ricky left the band after five years. Exhausted, he took some time to recoup before launching a solo career.

In 1999, he released "Livin' La Vida Loca," a song that would be heard blasting from stereos every summer for years to come.

Ten years later, Ricky became the father to two sons. He also came out as gay.

In a book titled *Me*, he spoke about how happy and relieved he was to finally come out. For years, people had pestered him with questions about whether he was gay and he hadn't felt quite ready to discuss it. It had made him feel lonely, but now that he'd opened up about it, he was grateful for all the love and support of the lesbian, gay, bisexual, and transgender (LGBT) community.

"I wish everyone that is struggling now could feel what I'm feeling," he said. "It's just love coming from every direction!"

Ricky isn't a Catholic any more, but he hasn't abandoned spirituality altogether. Sometimes he wears a t-shirt that reads: God is too big to fit into one religion.

XIUHTEZCATL MARTINEZ
(BORN 2000)

Xiuhtezcatl Martinez had been speaking out for what he believed in since he was six years old. Growing up surrounded by wildlife and the cultural traditions of his Aztec ancestors, he had always felt deeply connected to the environment.

Xiuhtezcatl would spend hours out in the forest with his father, searching for animals and coming to learn how parts of the earth were being destroyed as colossal companies chased bigger and bigger profits.

In July 2015, the United Nations held a conference on climate change and how to reverse the damage humans have inflicted on their natural surroundings. The room in Manhattan, New York, was packed full of middle-aged bureaucrats, dressed in suits and ties, tapping furiously on their phones. Then Xiuhtezcatl, who was fifteen, stood up to speak, his long hair flowing and his eyes glinting with determination.

"I stand before you representing my entire generation," he said. "Youth are standing up all over the world to find solutions."

Later that year, Xiuhtezcatl formed a group with twenty other kids and took the US government to court. They claimed that by ignoring climate change, the politicians were depriving young people of a right to life on a healthy planet.

Xiuhtezcatl also fights for change as part of the Earth Guardians, a group led by young people dedicated to creating a future we can all thrive in.

He raps his views, too. In 2015, the Earth Guardians song "Speak for the Trees" was chosen as the official song for the Paris Climate Change Conference. He sang:

"And some people turn away but I raise my voice and say

What will be left for my generation at the end of the day?"

In 2017, Xiuhtezcatl published a book titled *We Rise*, aimed at showing everyone how they could make a difference. He wants young people to stand up beside him and fight for the future of their home.

KIMANI MARUGE

(1920–2009)

In 2004, Kimani broke a world record. It wasn't for driving fast or eating a hundred hot dogs in one minute, but for being the oldest person ever to enroll in primary school. Kimani was eighty-four years old.

Kimani had always dreamed of being able to read the Bible on his own. Poverty and a lack of educational opportunities meant that felt like an impossible wish. His life was one of hard work and farming to get enough food to stay alive.

Then, as war gripped Kenya, Kimani fought in the Mau Mau Uprising, trying to free those detained by the British. He lost a foot and suffered torture at the hands of soldiers. For ten years, Kimani was imprisoned. When he was finally released, he married, had many children, and set about trying to rebuild his life.

That's when Kimani heard that the Kenyan government was finally making primary education free. He had a school uniform made in his size and turned up at the gates in shorts and long socks, with a backpack hanging off his shoulder. Some people were against him going to school with kids. Other people thought he was crazy.

Kimani didn't care. He knew that everyone has a right to an education and he was determined to get his, regardless of how old he was.

Soon, Kimani was able to read the Bible as he'd always dreamed of doing. And he read it every day.

Even when violence spread again and Kimani was forced to move to a refugee camp, he still walked 2.5 miles every day to attend school. A film called *The First Grader* was made of Kimani's life. He inspired people throughout Kenya and beyond to seek out opportunities for themselves and know that it's never too late to change, grow, and learn.

KYLIAN MBAPPÉ

(BORN 1998)

Kylian grew up in Bondy, a poor *banlieue* (suburb) of Paris, where crime was high and life tough. His father was the coach of the local soccer team, and some of the players can still remember a two-year-old Kylian wandering in and sitting down to listen in on their pre-match talks.

By the age of six, Kylian was filling his every spare minute with soccer. His bedroom was wallpapered with posters of Cristiano Ronaldo, and if he wasn't out playing, he was scoring goals across the living room or playing FIFA with his brother.

The other kids would laugh at the funny way Kylian ran, as his body was awkward and it always looked like he was leaving an arm behind. But it didn't matter. Kylian was so good that he had to spend most of his time playing with people twice his age to stop himself getting bored. Even at that age, he was confusing defenders with a kind of move the French call *passement de jambes*.

At sixteen, Kylian signed to Monaco. He became the youngest player ever to score for them, breaking the record previously held by Thierry Henry.

When he won the Under-19 final with France, all of Kylian's teammates went out to party. Not Kylian. He went straight home to sleep. Now he'd completed one goal, he was ready to set his sights on the next.

In the 2018 World Cup, Kylian became the first teenage soccer player to score multiple goals in the knock-out stages since Pelé did so back in the 1950s. He donated all the money he earned playing in the World Cup to a charity called Premiers de Cordée, which offers sports opportunities to children with disabilities.

Whenever Kylian scores, he poses with his arms crossed and his hands tucked into his armpits. It's the stance his brother used to take whenever he scored against Kylian on FIFA.

Today, a gigantic picture of Kylian has been painted onto the side of a building in Bondy. Behind him, the caption reads: Bondy, the city of possibilities.

CHRIS MOSIER

(BORN 1980)

The long-distance duathlon is a grueling sports event that involves running for 10 kilometers, cycling for 150 kilometers, and then running for another 30 kilometers. In 2016, Chris became the first openly transgender man to compete for America when he raced in the Duathlon World Championship.

It marked six years since he'd first transitioned, taking hormones and having surgery that would bring his body in line with the way he felt inside. Since the age of four, Chris had felt that his body was preventing him from getting close to other people and from showing who he really was. He'd been competing as a woman before transitioning, but the discomfort he'd felt at being in his own skin prevented him from being able to give his all. At the age of thirty, he finally felt ready to change that.

Chris knows he could have competed as a male athlete without ever having to tell the world he was born in a biologically female body. But he felt it was important to be honest.

"I think it makes a difference for young trans kids to see me as an athlete and know they can do it, too," he says. "I want to be the person I needed to be ten years ago."

For Chris, sports are tools that can bring about great change, both in those competing and those looking on from the sidelines. He hopes that trans athletes will continue to compete at the highest level in sports, and that their bodies will become facts irrelevant to the people they truly are.

Thanks in part to Chris's work, the International Olympic Committee have ruled that transgender athletes can now take part in Olympic events without restriction.

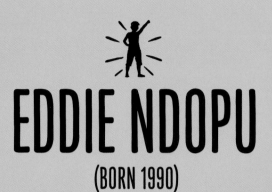

EDDIE NDOPU

(BORN 1990)

When he was born, Eddie was diagnosed with spinal muscular atrophy, a disease that causes people to gradually lose the ability to walk, eat, or breathe. He wasn't supposed to live past five years old. But in 2020, he's thirty and counting.

That's not the only expectation he's overturned.

In South Africa, almost all disabled people never see the inside of a classroom. Eddie was determined to get an education. That determination paid off when he found a small elementary school outside his hometown where the teachers were prepared to take him. From there, he went on to be selected for the African Leadership Academy, studied in Canada, and become involved with various global charities.

"I'm unapologetically brilliant, black, queer, and disabled," Eddie says. "I dwell in the magnificence of my difference."

In 2017, Eddie became the first African person with a disability to graduate from Oxford University after being awarded a full scholarship to study there. He hopes it can act as proof to disabled young people

everywhere that there is nothing they can't accomplish.

Eddie wants everyone to forget the negative things they've been taught about what it means to be disabled and to embrace it as part of themselves. He says: "There's no reason why disability can't be sexy, genius, cool."

Eddie loves lipstick, fashion, and Beyoncé.

His mission isn't just to install more wheelchair ramps and braille signs, but to have disabled people be seen for the people they are, and for them to be offered the same opportunities as everyone else.

Eddie's next plan? He wants to become the first wheelchair user in space, so that the people of planet Earth can prove that they're not going to leave anyone behind.

ĀPIRANA NGATA

(1874–1950)

When white European settlers began colonizing New Zealand in the nineteenth century, the Māori people had already been living there for more than eight hundred years. The new arrivals brought foreign diseases and fought with the native people over the land.

As more European settlers arrived, the Māori population shrank. It seemed as though their language and way of life might be in danger of disappearing. Āpirana was set on changing that.

He was born one of fifteen children in the small town of Kawakawa. He received a traditional Māori education and spoke the language, but his father, a tribal leader, believed that in order for their people to flourish, they would have to learn to coexist with the more recent arrivals. Āpirana was the first Māori to complete a degree at a New Zealand university.

Āpirana became a respected leader and was looked to for guidance when it became clear the white settlers were breaking the terms of a treaty they had signed many years before.

In government, he spoke out against the government's attempts to sell Māori land. He also called for support of traditional Māori arts.

But Āpirana also clashed with tradition sometimes. He supported a government bill that would replace traditional healers with modern medical doctors.

On the one-hundred-year anniversary of the treaty signed between the Māori and the white settlers, Āpirana stood and gave a speech. He said, "Lands gone, the power of chiefs humbled in the dust, Māori culture scattered and broken. What remained of all the fine things said one hundred years ago?"

He would never stop fighting for the survival of his people, and for this, Āpirana has been hailed by many as the greatest Māori ever.

Thanks to the fearless work of people like Āpirana, the New Zealand government has taken steps toward compensating Māori people and creating projects and schemes to preserve and encourage their language and culture.

EMMANUEL OFOSU YEBOAH

(BORN 1977)

Emmanuel was born with no shinbone in his right leg.
It meant his foot dangled uselessly and he had no hope
of ever walking normally.

In Ghana, people are often suspicious of those who are born disabled, believing it to be the result of a curse or the mother having sinned. Emmanuel's father had even left the family to escape the shame.

Comfort Yeboah, Emmanuel's mother, insisted that he would have every opportunity in life. Even though disabled children in Ghana almost never went to school, she would carry him the entire four miles (seven kilometers) each day until he was old enough to hop there on his own. It was expected that, as a disabled person, Emmanuel would become a beggar. But he had other ideas.

Emmanuel wanted to ride a bike across the whole of Ghana using only one leg. The problem was, he didn't have a bike. He put together a letter to the Challenged Athletes Foundation in America, who wrote back, offering him a special mountain bike, cycling gear, and $1,000.

Along his 372-mile (600-kilometer) journey, Emmanuel met the King of

Ghana, villagers, reporters, church leaders, and disabled children. He wanted to show his country that disability does not mean inability, that it is not a curse or a punishment, and that those born disabled are capable of wondrous things.

"In this world, we are not perfect," says Emmanuel. "We can only do our best."

He was then invited to America to compete in a triathlon. While he was there, he met specialist doctors, who explained they could amputate his leg and fit him with a prosthetic one. It was a roaring success. Emmanuel could walk on his own two feet.

The prosthetic also allowed him to beat his own personal best triathlon time by three hours. For that, Emmanuel was awarded the Nike Casey Martin Award, which came with $50,000. Back in Ghana, he used it to set up a fund to help disabled children access the education that had helped him to thrive.

ARYAN PASHA

(BORN 1991)

Aryan was born in India and first given the name Nayla. Although he was born in the body of a girl, he knew it didn't fit with how he felt inside. Aryan was six when he first told his parents that he wasn't going to school unless he got to wear the boys' uniform. They accepted it, and soon he was known as a boy by his friends in school.

Still, things were difficult. Aryan loved ice-skating but he had to compete alongside girls, which made him feel out of place. He also preferred to use the boys' toilets but had to be careful in case anyone questioned him. He was bullied and threatened at school.

As he was growing up, Aryan's stepmother, who had studied psychology, noticed him becoming angry, depressed, and lonely. She told him about transgender people: about how sometimes people could be born with heads and hearts that didn't match the gender of their bodies. Aryan was relieved to have some understanding of his situation and to know it wasn't something that only he was going through.

But things didn't improve at school, and he soon dropped out. At eighteen, he went through serious surgeries that changed his body from female to male.

The changes left him far happier than he'd ever been before. Finally, he had a body that matched how he felt inside. He changed his name to Aryan.

Aryan became a lawyer and went on to work for an organization that fights for the rights of lesbian, gay, bisexual, and transgender (LGBT) people in India. In 2014, a law was passed in India giving transgender people the same rights as everyone else. Part of Aryan's work is to make sure that law is enforced.

These days, Aryan spends a lot of his time bodybuilding. It gives him confidence and helps him feel at home in his own skin. Soon, he's going to open his own chain of gyms so he can help other people feel the same way.

OLIVER PERCOVICH

(BORN 1974)

Growing up in Papua New Guinea, Oliver would entertain himself by skateboarding in an empty pool. Years later, after moving to Afghanistan to be with his girlfriend, Oliver took out his skateboard again for a ride around the city's streets.

He was amazed by the excitement of the children he passed, particularly the girls. They would chase after him, curious about the board under his feet, and ask whether they could have a go on it. Oliver quickly realized the potential skating had to unite them. In a country where 50 percent of the population was under fifteen years old, giving kids something positive to care about was vital.

It was also a huge chance for girls to get involved with sports. Because skateboarding was so new to Afghanistan, there were no preconceived ideas about who should or shouldn't be engaging in the sport. For years, girls had been taught that they couldn't play soccer, fly kites, or ride bikes, but no one had ever told them anything about skateboarding. Many of them fell in love with it.

Oliver started collecting donations and setting up skate sessions with children from across the city. He found that by skating together, the kids learned to trust each other, regardless of gender, ethnicity, or how rich their families were.

To keep the momentum going, Oliver founded a charity called Skateistan. The group wanted to engage kids with sports as well as help them gain an education, get involved in the creative arts, and learn leadership skills.

Skateboarding has now become the most popular sport for girls in Afghanistan. In a country ranked one of the worst places in the world to be a woman, skateboarding has given girls the chance to feel free.

Skateistan has since spread beyond Afghanistan, building skateboard parks in South Africa and Cambodia. They aim to give kids the skills needed to transform their lives.

MICHAEL PHELPS

(BORN 1985)

As a boy, Michael was diagnosed with attention deficit hyperactivity disorder (ADHD). It meant he was filled with energy and found it difficult to concentrate or control his liveliness. Luckily, he found an outlet for all that vitality in the swimming pool.

Michael was scared to put his face under the water at first. Once he got over it, he proved himself a natural swimmer. A huge wing span, extremely flexible ankles, and an unbelievable amount of determination soon saw Michael competing at the highest level.

In the 2008 Olympic Games, Michael swam so well that people thought he was cheating. Nine tests later, he proved he wasn't.

He went on to become the most decorated Olympian in history with a total of twenty-eight medals earned over the course of five Olympic Games.

But between the grand moments of glory, Michael was struggling with his own mind. Overwhelming waves of despair would leave him feeling so unhappy that he sometimes didn't want to live anymore.

In a treatment center, Michael learned how to speak about and understand his emotions. He realized that it was okay not to be okay, as long as you didn't try to bottle it up and could be honest with the people around you.

Since then, Michael has stopped competing to focus his efforts on running a charity that helps young people find meaning through swimming, as well as campaigning for mental health and encouraging everyone to speak up about how they feel.

Does he miss swimming?

Not really. Michael once said, "Those moments and those feelings and those emotions for me are lightyears better than winning the gold medal."

JYOTIRAO PHULE

(1827–1890)

Jyotirao was born a Dalit in India, which meant he was an Untouchable. An Untouchable cannot live within a higher caste village, eat or drink in the same room as a member of a higher caste, touch a member of a higher caste, or take water from the same well as those from a higher caste. The only jobs available to Untouchables involve preparing dead bodies, cleaning toilets, or killing rats.

Jyotirao was very lucky. Although he was supposed to have stopped education early on, his neighbors, a Muslim on one side and a Christian on the other, convinced his father to let him continue. Jyotirao was made to marry a thirteen-year-old girl, as was the custom at the time. Because he knew how important learning was, he secretly taught her to read and write. He was kicked out by his family because of it.

Together with his wife, Savitribai, Jyotirao created the first Indian school for girls as well as schools for those from Untouchable castes. He opened his house to Untouchables and invited them to use his well. He urged the government to pass laws that promoted equality and made primary education compulsory in all villages. Such a law wouldn't be passed until over a hundred years later, in 2009.

Despite the reforms made possible by Jyotirao's work, Dalits still face extreme discrimination today. They are not allowed to touch food or water in schools, not allowed in temples, made to sit at the back of classrooms, and sometimes are even beaten up by teachers. However, there are more girls than ever being educated in India, and we have Jyotirao and Savitribai to thank for kick-starting that.

JACKSON POLLOCK

(1912–1956)

Jackson's parents died within a year of each other and he was adopted by his foster parents. He was expelled from one school and then from another.

Jackson was very unhappy as a teenager. He stood out for having long hair and dressing differently. In one letter, he wrote, "People have always frightened and bored me and consequently I have been within my own shell."

Jackson found that what he truly cared about was painting and nature. He loved the connection that Native American art showed to the natural world.

While living in New York, Jackson was so poor he often had to steal food and gas to survive. At that time, he was painting strange, surreal pictures filled with symbols and curious figures.

In the 1940s, Jackson came up with the technique that would make him known across the world. Instead of carefully painted shapes, Jackson wanted something that was more fluid and more alive with movement. He wanted a means of expression that came from the gut. And so the "drip technique" was created.

Paint would be flung, dropped, and spattered across canvases. Jackson would dance around the canvas as he threw on the paint. In that way, he felt he could immerse himself in the picture he was creating and become a part of it, the same way that Native American sand painters in the west of America had done.

Opinions were split over Jackson's art. One magazine asked, "Is he the greatest living painter in the United States?" While another claimed, "This is not art—it's a joke in bad taste."

Jackson fell in love, married, and moved out to the countryside. He turned to sculpture but spent a lot of time struggling with his mental health and trying to control his drinking. Sixty years later, one of Jackson's paintings was sold for $200 million. He is now recognized as a revolutionary painter who redefined the creative process.

PRINCE HARRY

(BORN 1984)

On August 31, 1997, Princess Diana of Wales was killed in a car crash. Her two sons, William and Harry, were left grieving for their mother. As millions of people around the world watched on television, the two young princes were made to walk along behind her coffin. It was a harrowing experience that would never leave either of them.

Harry struggled with academic work at school but found his calling in sports. He signed up to attend Sandhurst military academy. Once he'd graduated, there was some debate about whether he should be allowed to fight. Harry put his foot down. "There's no way I'll sit on my bottom while my boys are out fighting for their country," he announced.

After serving in Afghanistan, Harry set up the Invictus Games, an international sporting event for wounded or sick army personnel. He also directed his energy into supporting charities involved with children, education, rain forests, poaching, and human rights, among various others.

At the age of thirty-two, Harry felt comfortable enough to reveal how difficult life inside his own head had been in the years after his mother had died. He explained that he'd shut down all emotions rather than deal with the grief, and that had led to anger and anxiety building up inside him.

"People are scared to talk about it," he said. "But they should be scared to not talk about it."

He hoped that by opening up about his own experiences, he'd give others the courage to do the same.

In 2016, Harry met an American actress named Meghan Markle on a blind date. They fell deeply in love and, in 2018, over a billion people across the world tuned in to watch their wedding. Instead of gifts, Harry and Meghan asked people to donate to the charities that were closest to their hearts, including one for children of the Armed Forces who have lost parents in the line of duty.

LEE RIDLEY

(BORN 1980)

When Lee took to the *Britain's Got Talent* stage in 2018, no one knew what to expect. Singing? Dancing? Magic? Lee introduced himself as Lost Voice Guy. With the aid of a talking computer, he went on to tell jokes that had millions of people throughout Britain laughing until their sides hurt.

The crowd gave him a standing ovation. Judges called him the best stand-up comedian they'd ever seen.

Lee had been diagnosed with cerebral palsy when he was six months old. It's a condition that affects a person's ability to control their muscles and can lead to problems with vision, hearing, speech, and learning. After two months in a coma, he'd been left unable to develop the power of speech. He felt isolated until his eighth birthday, when Lee was first given a computerized way of communicating.

His parents say he never let his condition hold him back. Often, he'd use humor as a kind of shield. "If I didn't laugh," he said, "I would most definitely cry."

He loved doing impressions. When he grew up, he quit his job to pursue comedy full time. It paid off when the votes started pouring in on *Britain's Got Talent*.

A few days before the final, Lee fell and injured himself in his hotel room. His fans were shocked to see him with a bruised face. As ever, Lee saw the funny side. "This is why Lost Balance Guy never made it on *Britain's Got Talent*," he wrote.

But Lee went on to win the competition, earning him more than $250,000 and a chance to perform for the queen.

At the moment, there is no known cure for cerebral palsy. "My disability has certainly got me more coverage that I would have without it," Lee has joked. "Let's hope they never find a cure for me!"

RAINER MARIA RILKE

(1875–1926)

Rainer's mother had lost a baby girl named Sophie and often tried to turn her son into a replacement daughter by dressing him in skirts. She would call him Sophie and insist that he played with dolls.

As a result, Rainer felt all his life that he was not the child his mother had wanted. Instead, he found comfort in writing, but his parents sent him to a military school at the age of ten where he was bullied.

Once he'd finished school, Rainer traveled the world, never staying in one place for long. He went to Russia, Germany, Spain, Austria, Italy, Egypt, and Tunisia, never quite finding a place to call home.

While traveling, Rainer met Princess Marie of Thurn and Taxis, who offered him her castle to work in. It was a relief for him to have somewhere safe at a time when he often felt lost and despondent.

In his poems, Rainer sought a meaning for life as well as an outlet for expressing the turmoil he felt within himself. Rainer also wrote letters about life and love to people around the world. He penned ten such letters to a young cadet at a military academy,

passages from which are still quoted today for their insight and wisdom.

In one, he wrote about what can help someone become an author: "What you really need is simply this— aloneness, great inner solitude . . . To be lonely as one was lonely as a child, while adults were moving about, entangled with things that seemed big and important, because the grown-ups looked so busy and because one could not understand any of their doings— that must be the goal."

Rainer lived his entire life in service to poetry. For him, the goal was always to express himself as beautifully, as honestly, and as forcefully as possible, and in doing so form bonds and connections with people of the present and future. He remains one of the world's bestselling poets and a writer people still turn to in times of need.

HRITHIK ROSHAN

(BORN 1974)

As a boy, Hrithik hated talking. He had a stammer that would cause him to panic whenever he was supposed to be saying something in front of people. He also had an extra thumb, fused onto the thumb of his right hand, which marked him as more different and caused other kids at school to be cruel.

At the age of six, Hrithik had a small part dancing in a Bollywood film. He earned enough to buy ten Hot Wheels cars. He fell in love with acting and became set on one day becoming a professional Bollywood actor.

With the help of therapy, Hrithik overcame his stammer. It wasn't the only obstacle put in his way. A few years later, he was diagnosed with scoliosis, which means his spine is curved. The doctor told Hrithik he wouldn't be able to perform vigorous movements. For a Bollywood actor, not being able to dance would mean not being able to work at all, as almost all Bollywood films are packed with high-energy songs and stunts. Hrithik decided to pursue acting as a career anyway. One evening he ran along a beach as it poured with rain, realized he felt no pain, and understood that he could achieve his dream.

He turned down a scholarship to study in America and threw himself into the film business instead. On film sets, Hrithik swept floors and made tea, intent on learning the industry from the bottom up.

Finally, he earned a part in a romantic thriller called *Say . . . You're in Love*. The film was a hit. Overnight, Hrithik became one of the most famous actors in India. Everyone was clamoring to work with him.

Since becoming successful, Hrithik has used his money to help kids who are in the same boat that he once was. He supports a school for mentally challenged children, donates to a hospital that aims to help kids who stammer, and helped rebuild homes after floods decimated South India.

ERNÖ RUBIK

(BORN 1944)

Growing up, Ernö was always inspired by his dad, who worked as an engineer crafting gliders—planes that fly using only the wind. His dad taught him that if he wanted something done, he could do it with his own two hands.

In college, Ernö studied sculpture before going on to become a professor of architecture at Budapest College of Applied Arts in Hungary. It frustrated him that his students found it so difficult to conquer certain 3-D problems vital to their studies. He decided to come up with a new, interactive way for them to learn.

Back in his mother's apartment, Ernö got to work creating the very first Rubik's Cube. He cut blocks of wood, painted them, and fixed them together with elastic bands. He then twisted the cube into a completely random arrangement of colors.

After turning the cube over and over, Ernö started to wonder if it would be possible to solve it and get the colors back to where they'd originally been. He worked out that there were forty-three quintillion possible arrangements. It meant that if you could see a thousand of them every second, it would still take thirteen

hundred million years to see every single one. It took Ernö a month to solve his own puzzle and get the colors on each side to match up. He started to believe it might have potential as a toy.

It was difficult to convince a company to manufacture the cube. It didn't light up or spin or fire rubber pellets—all it involved was a lot of sitting and thinking. But the toy companies had underestimated young people.

The Rubik's Cube became the most popular toy in the world. It is estimated that one in every seven people alive today has played with one. It even spawned its own sport, speedcubing, where participants attempt to solve a Rubik's Cube as quickly as possible. The current record stands at 4.22 seconds.

Rubik's Cubes have inspired generations of young people to fall in love with puzzles, problems, and the quest for answers.

EVAN RUGGIERO

(BORN 1990)

Evan started dancing at five. Ever since peeking into his sister's dance class, he had been captivated. At first, he danced hip-hop and jazz, but when he discovered tap, Evan knew what he wanted to spend the rest of his life doing.

When Evan was nineteen and studying musical theatre in college, he was diagnosed with a rare form of bone cancer in his leg. The leg had to be amputated below the knee, and Evan went through sixteen months of grueling chemotherapy.

Nobody knew if he'd be able to dance again.

But Evan was inspired by the story of "Peg Leg" Bates, an African American dancer from the 1940s who lost his leg at the age of twelve and went on to dance for the king and queen of England. Bates had been told he could dance better with one leg than most dancers could with two.

A week after his chemotherapy was finished, Evan strapped on a peg leg and headed to the dance studio. He wanted to see what he was capable of. He was amazed. In the coming months and years, Evan would learn how best to use his new body as an instrument of expression, and he would flourish.

It wasn't always easy, but Evan said he'd had plenty of practice overcoming obstacles. Growing up as a boy who loved musical theatre meant that he'd already spent years contending with bullies. He was used to dealing with problems, and it had never slowed him down before.

Evan has since performed at the Paralympics, the Oscars, and in various roles on Broadway. "I didn't choose any of this," he said. "But my career will probably be bigger and better because of my peg leg."

OLIVER SACKS

(1933–2015)

Oliver dealt with extreme shyness all his life. He believed it was a result of having a brain disorder called face blindness, which leaves the sufferer unable to recognize or remember faces. Oliver couldn't even recognize his own reflection in the mirror. It would be his first introduction to the bizarre world of brain disorders.

Growing up in a family of physicians, Oliver was exposed to science from an early age. But he and his brother were evacuated from home for four years during the Second World War while London was being bombed. They wound up having to live with a cruel family who would barely feed them. Once he returned home, Oliver dedicated himself to chemistry and discovered an interest in medicine, finally moving to America to continue his studies.

Once there, Oliver went wild, became a bodybuilder, and tore around on a motorcycle. One day, he decided to give it all up to focus on exploring the brain. He became a professor of neurology at Albert Einstein College of Medicine. Then he started writing the books that would make his name known throughout the world.

Using his own cases, Oliver put together thrilling accounts of abnormal brains. He described a patient who could walk, talk, and think normally but mistook his own wife for a hat. He wrote about a Micronesian island where everyone saw in black and white. He chronicled a man living in the 1980s whose memory had frozen during the Second World War, meaning he still thought he was in 1945.

To ensure his work continued after he was gone, Oliver established the Oliver Sacks Foundation, dedicated to helping the human race learn more about the mysteries of the brain.

At the age of eighty-one, Oliver discovered he had cancer. In an essay saying goodbye to the world, he wrote, "I have been a sentient being, a thinking animal, on this beautiful planet, and that in itself has been an enormous privilege and adventure."

YVES SAINT LAURENT

(1936–2008)

Yves grew up in a beautiful house on the Mediterranean Sea, though his early years were difficult and lonely. At school, he was bullied for being gay, small, and shy. The only thing that gave him joy was fashion. He'd spend hours going through magazines, sketching his own designs, and making dresses for his mother and sisters.

Yves won an international competition when he was eighteen and was hired by the biggest name in fashion, Christian Dior. He moved to Paris and threw himself headfirst into the glamorous world of fashion.

When his mentor died, Yves was thrust into the spotlight. He didn't know what to make of the attention, and the media didn't know what to make of him. One magazine wrote that he was "so horribly shy he couldn't take his eyes off the floor."

His first collection with the fashion house was a raging success. The next two were not, and Yves was cast aside. It was such a blow that Yves struggled to cope and was admitted to a mental hospital.

It would be up to a man named Pierre Bergé to get him out.

Once he did, the two men would found the Yves Saint Laurent fashion house together, as well as spend the following years falling in and out of love with each other.

Yves's first release on his own label was the Mondrian dress, a revolutionary, loose-hanging dress influenced by the work of modern artists.

The next year, Yves drew inspiration from men's clothes for the garments he made for women. He unveiled to the world the Le Smoking tuxedo suit. Strong women everywhere adopted it as a symbol of rebellion. When one famous New York socialite wasn't allowed into a restaurant because she was wearing the suit rather than a dress, she whipped off the trousers in response, trying to highlight how ridiculous such rules were.

It has been said that "Coco Chanel liberated women, but Yves Saint Laurent gave them power."

JOEL SALINAS

(BORN 1983)

Every time Joel watched television, he went on a roller-coaster of emotions. When a character jumped for joy, he would feel an equal thrill in his heart. When another was hit by a truck, he would feel that pain inside him, too. Joel has a condition called mirror-touch synesthesia.

The condition means that whenever he sees someone else feeling a sensation, emotional or physical, Joel feels that sensation, too. It makes hugging particularly intense. At school, Joel tried to hug the other kids so much that they thought he was weird. Feeling rejected, he'd spend more and more time in front of the television.

As he grew older, Joel realized that what he enjoyed most was healing people. Not only would helping others make them happier, but his condition meant it would make him happier, too. He became determined to qualify as a doctor.

Medical school was difficult. Whenever students had to operate on someone, Joel would feel the knife slicing him open, too. When someone died, Joel found himself in the bathroom being sick.

But his condition had upsides. Joel was so in tune with his patients that he could pick up on tiny symptoms. He could tell when they were dehydrated or nauseous or struggling to breathe, because he would feel those things right along with them.

Joel has written a book about his experiences. He currently practices medicine at Massachusetts General Hospital as well as conducts research into different aspects of the human brain.

His condition can make life difficult, though Joel would never change a thing.

"Because I get to be a part of some of this pain and suffering," he says, "the patients get to be a little less alone, and that means a lot in medicine."

BUN SALUTH

(BORN 1970)

Bun Saluth was born into a poor farming family in Cambodia. He knew from an early age that he wanted to become a Buddhist monk. For five years, he studied in Thailand. There, he learned not just about Buddhism, but also about the environment.

Thailand had lost almost two-thirds of its trees to logging. In 1936, 70 percent of the country had been covered in forest. By 1989, it had fallen to around 20 percent. The loss of trees had led to devastating floods that destroyed whole villages and claimed thousands of lives.

Bun Saluth resolved to prevent the same thing from happening in Cambodia.

He moved into a large forest near where he'd grown up.

At first, Bun Saluth lived there alone. Then people began arriving and establishing villages. They chopped down trees without being aware of the consequences. Temperatures rose. Rainfall became unpredictable.

Bun Saluth knew he had to do something. With other monks, he dug a ditch around the entire forest.

He worked at trying to educate the villagers on the importance of preserving the trees. Instead of chopping down the ancient trees, he encouraged them to forage for mushrooms, catch fish, or gather fruit. They disapproved at first, thinking it would be better to invite in the money that logging would bring. But soon enough, the effects caused by deforestation were undeniable even to them.

Now the villagers work together with Bun Saluth, patrolling the forest to stop those who seek to destroy it. They don't have any official powers. Instead, if they come across any illegal activity, the guardians of the forest try to teach the loggers why what they're doing is wrong and how it hurts us all.

Why does he do it? Bun Saluth said, "I got involved with climate change, because if I didn't do it, who else would?"

ED SHEERAN

(BORN 1991)

After moving to London with a guitar and a backpack full of clothes, Ed found himself homeless. For two years, he slept on trains, on friends' floors, and even next to a heating duct outside Buckingham Palace.

He wasn't about to give up on his dream of becoming a singer.

Since the age of eleven, Ed had been set on a career in music. He'd been singing in a choir since he was four, and music had always offered a release and an escape from the bullying he was subjected to at school. Having a lazy eye, a stutter, red hair, and giant glasses meant other kids would pick on him mercilessly. Speech therapy wasn't helping to improve his talking, and it frustrated Ed endlessly to have words in his head and be unable to get them out.

It was rap music that cured him. One day, his dad accidentally bought Ed an Eminem album. Soon Ed had learned every word to every rap. His stutter had gone.

Ed left home at fourteen and moved to London. He put everything he could into making music work, sometimes playing up to three hundred gigs a year.

Eventually, people started noticing the boy with the beat-up guitar and scruffy red hair. Ed had a way of blending elements of his favorite musical styles—from folk to rap— into an infectious kind of pop that people couldn't help singing and dancing along to.

Four years later, Ed was invited back to Buckingham Palace to perform for the queen. He's since held the record for the fastest-selling album ever by a male artist, which sold one hundred million singles, been awarded an MBE (The Most Excellent Order of the British Empire, a British order of chivalry rewarding contributions to the arts and sciences), and married a girl he'd fallen in love with back at school.

Part of the reason for his success? Never changing who he was. "Be yourself," Ed says. "Embrace your quirks. Being weird is a wonderful thing."

RENE SILVA

(BORN 1994)

The favelas of Brazil are poor areas around large cities where people have built their own houses. Most don't have sewage systems or drinking water, making them difficult and dangerous places to live. For Rene Silva, the Alemão favela outside Rio de Janeiro is home.

Rene was just eleven when he decided to do something that would help his community. Using the computers at school, he created a newspaper called *Voz da Comunidade*, which translates as *Community Voice* in English. The first issue consisted of one hundred copies.

With money from advertisements, Rene grew the paper until each issue was selling over three thousand copies. The paper became big enough to raise money for computers and webcams. Using this new technology, Rene aimed to give the people of his neighborhood a voice they'd never had before.

In 2011, the Brazilian government sent its army storming through the favelas in search of criminals. Rene had let the residents know what was going on.

Years later, the government took over various favelas once again. This time, they wanted to evict people from their homes and demolish the buildings.

As no foreign journalists were allowed nearby, it was Rene who almost instantly managed to get word to the wider world about the treatment his people were receiving at the hands of their government.

While he was taking pictures, police pepper-sprayed Rene, handcuffed him, and dragged him away. He tried to explain that, as a member of the press, he had a right to document what was going on. They wouldn't listen.

To this day, Rene works to help the people of his favela through psychological support, language courses, and work programs. In 2018, he was named one of the most influential people of African descent in the world. The newspaper he started at the age of eleven now has almost half a million followers on social media.

LEOPOLD SOCHA

(1909–1946)

Leopold was an orphan who had led a hard life and spent most of his years as a petty criminal. He was a sewage worker when the Nazis came to occupy his city of Lviv, in the Ukraine.

The Nazis forced the Jewish residents of Lviv into a smaller and smaller area, called a ghetto. One day, a Jewish carpenter named Ignacy Chiger realized that they were about to clear out the ghetto and kill those in it. He took his family down into the sewer to hide.

That was where they were discovered by Leopold, who agreed to help the family in return for money.

The Chigers lived among rats, maggots, and the constant flow of raw, stinking sewage. They never saw the sky and were so close to the surface that they had to speak in whispers.

Soon, the family ran out of money. Leopold, his wife, and his friend managed to pool their resources and help them with what little they had.

Leopold went from helping the family for money to helping them from the goodness of his heart, even though it put him at risk of death. It was difficult.

Their drinking water had to be fetched from a fountain many miles away and food was already scarce for everyone in the city.

The Chigers' children came to see Leopold as a second father. He would sit with them for hours, talking, teaching, and answering questions. Their mother believed he was an angel sent by God to look after them.

Once the city had been set free by the Russians and Leopold was sure it was safe, he helped the Chiger family out of the sewer. They'd been underground for fourteen months.

One year after the end of the war, Leopold and his daughter were out riding bikes when an army truck came heading straight for them. Leopold managed to knock his daughter out of the way of the truck, but he died in the process, saving one more life.

SOCRATES

(DIED 399 BC)

There's a lot we don't know about Socrates for certain. We know he was probably born between 471 and 468 BC. We know he wandered the streets of ancient Athens barefoot, debating with anyone who would speak to him. And we know he went on to be called the Father of Western Philosophy, despite being sentenced to death.

Instead of looking to gods, Socrates looked to people. He believed happiness was not something given by the heavens, which is what people believed at the time, but something that could be achieved through human effort. The way to happiness, according to Socrates, lay in pursuing love, friendship, and community, rather than in chasing money and possessions.

To deal with the big issues of good and evil, happiness, truth, and courage, Socrates came up with the Socratic method. It involved asking a series of questions that would move the philosopher closer and closer to some kind of truth. It is a method that has been widely used ever since.

Socrates was certain he knew nothing. He said it was understanding how little he knew that made him so much wiser than other people.

Eventually, Socrates was put on trial for corrupting the youth of Athens and sentenced to death by drinking a poison called hemlock.

Socrates had many friends and admirers who offered to help him break out of jail. He turned them all away, claiming that he could not go against the wishes of the community, as to do so would go against his own teachings.

In the years after Socrates' death, his teachings were written down by Plato, taught by Plato to Aristotle, and communicated by Aristotle to Alexander the Great, who went on to spread them across an empire that spanned three continents.

This was the beginning of Western philosophy. It posed questions that are still being discussed and debated in schools and universities today.

MATTIE STEPANEK

(1990–2004)

Mattie was born with dysautonomic mitochondrial myopathy. It is an illness that affects almost every function of the body, from heart rate to digestion to breathing.

Mattie's older sister and brothers—Katie, Stevie, and Jamie, who suffered from the same condition—all died before the age of four. Thanks to the progress in medical developments, Mattie survived for longer.

Several years after Jamie passed away, Mattie found poetry was the best way of capturing, expressing, and sharing his feelings with the world. His first collection, *Heartsongs*, won a national prize. It was so called because Mattie believed that every person has a purpose within them, and that these purposes are called "heartsongs."

His books of poems would go on to sell millions of copies and inspire millions of people to be thoughtful, grateful, and peace-loving.

"We all have life storms," he wrote in one. "And instead of just suffering through them, and then afterwards just sitting, crying and waiting to be wiped out by the next one, we should celebrate together that we got through."

When he wasn't writing, Mattie liked studying, reading, and practicing martial arts. He even earned a black belt in Hapkido. When Mattie got to meet his hero, President Jimmy Carter, it was the president who came away the more impressed of the two, calling Mattie the most extraordinary person he'd ever met.

Mattie died in 2004 at the age of thirteen. A foundation was set up in his name, a park named after him was opened in Maryland, and a huge performance of his poems set to music by an orchestra and a choir took place in Carnegie Hall.

Mattie once said, "I want to be remembered as a poet, a peacemaker and a philosopher who played."

And that's exactly how he will be remembered.

SATOSHI TAJIRI

(BORN 1965)

Satoshi has Asperger's syndrome, meaning he's on the autistic spectrum. He's known around the world but prefers not to speak about it in public. Actually, his Asperger's means he prefers not to really speak in public at all.

His condition meant that Satoshi grew up obsessing over certain things. At first, this obsession took the form of bug collecting. Satoshi would roam the countryside around his house, gathering all the bugs and insects he could find and studying them closely to learn more. His classmates even called him Mr. Bug.

As he grew older, his obsessions changed. Satoshi became infatuated with arcade games and would spend hours and hours playing *Space Invaders*. He played so often he almost didn't graduate from high school. It scared his parents into finding him a job at a power station. Satoshi turned down the job.

Instead, he went to a technology college to learn about electronics. There, Satoshi met Ken Sugimori and they created a gaming magazine together. The magazine was called *Game Freak*. Satoshi would write, and Ken would illustrate.

Then one day, Satoshi had an idea for a game. He wanted to capture the excitement he'd once felt when collecting bugs and offer it to children everywhere. He wanted to give them an open world to explore and lead adventures in. He wanted to give them the game he'd always wished for himself.

For six years, Satoshi and Ken worked tirelessly. Most of their staff quit, and Satoshi spent all of his savings and was forced to move back in with his dad.

Finally, it was ready.

Pokémon went on to become one of the biggest games the world has ever seen. For years, it's thrilled children all over. More recently, *Pokémon Go* has seen children and adults alike venturing out into the real world in search of bizarre and magical creatures.

FRANCISCO TÁRREGA

(1852–1909)

One night, while Francisco was being looked after by his nanny in Villarreal, Spain, he screamed so loud that she threw him into the canal. He was rescued but had contracted an infection that would severely affect his sight.

Wanting to make sure his son always had work despite his disability, Francisco's father encouraged him to become a musician. It wasn't a huge surprise to see him take to the idea. Francisco had always been in awe of the sounds his father could make while playing flamenco on his guitar. He studied under two local blind guitar players. But he was restless.

The first time Francisco ran away, he was ten. He was found playing in bars and cafés throughout Barcelona and brought home by his father.

The second time Francisco ran away, he was thirteen. His father found him in Valencia with a group of gypsies.

The third time Francisco ran away, he stayed away, going on to study guitar seriously at the Madrid Conservatory.

He received formal instruction in theory, composition, and piano, and began teaching as well as giving impressive concerts throughout Spain. His name was soon known far and wide.

Francisco changed how people thought of the guitar. Whereas before it had been used generally to accompany singers, Francisco proved that it was an instrument of beauty and power that could be used to play even the most complex classical compositions by Beethoven or Chopin. He also left behind a large number of his own compositions.

At the height of its popularity, an excerpt of Francisco's song was heard by two billion people every day: his music was used as the first Nokia ringtone.

BART WEETJENS

(BORN 1967)

Since he was a boy, Bart has loved rats. He kept them as pets and would train them to find treats for fun. Bart could never have predicted how many lives his unconventional passion would save.

Once he'd grown up and was studying at the University of Antwerp, Bart saw a documentary about the horrific number of deaths caused by leftover landmines, and how years after wars have ended, they can still be lying active on the ground, disguised as rocks or plants, waiting to be stepped on by unsuspecting civilians. Since 1975, over a million people have died that way. An estimated one hundred million landmines remain scattered throughout the world.

Bart was struck with an idea. What if his beloved rats could be trained to sniff out landmines as well as treats?

APOPO was created, which in English means Anti-Personnel Landmines Detection Product Development. Research began in Belgium and later shifted to Tanzania, Africa. Rats were soon found to be far quicker at detecting landmines than any other method of doing so. They were also so light they could stand on mines without setting them off.

Amazingly, Bart also discovered the rats could detect tuberculosis far more accurately than other methods. In developing countries, TB is a huge problem, with almost two million people dying from it each year. The rats proved they could uncover 40 percent more cases of the disease than traditional tests.

"There's a powerful and life-saving alert system in the little noses of these rats," Bart says. "Even after twenty years of working with them I'm still in awe of what they can do."

He has changed the opinions of many African people who once saw rats as pests and now see them as friends and helpers. That pleases Bart, who, as a Zen Buddhist priest, has great respect for all life.

APOPO continues to grow and spread, helping more and more people around the world. Supporters aid the organization by adopting hero rats (who go on to save lives).

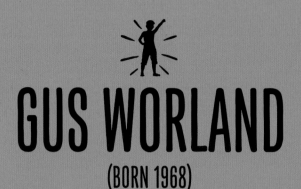

GUS WORLAND

(BORN 1968)

Gus was playing golf when he got a phone call that he never expected to receive. One of his best friends, Angus, had died by suicide. Gus fell to his knees and cried.

Gus went on to discover that suicide is the biggest killer of young men in Australia. If it was such a serious problem, he wondered, why did it seem as though nothing was being done about it?

As he was a star of television and radio in Australia, Gus decided he wanted to use the media to try and spread awareness and try to reach those who need help. He created a three-part documentary called *Man Up!* in an attempt to understand why it was that so many men were dying.

In the show, Gus spoke with builders on a building site, sailed with sailors, and joined in with a male yoga class. He learned that most of all, men have trouble being honest about how they're doing. If they don't seek out the help that's available, all of the worries they've kept inside can become overwhelming. Men who'd seen the documentary reported feeling more comfortable expressing themselves and more likely to think about the feelings of other people. It was an

amazing response and one Gus wanted to continue generating.

To do this, he created a nationwide commercial that showed men of various ages looking into the camera and crying.

Why do we tell boys not to cry? it asked. To harden up? To hide their emotions? Silence can kill, Gus says. Holding in emotions and bottling up problems can lead to anxiety, depression, and destructive outbursts. It takes a man to cry and strength to ask for help.

At home, Gus also tries to encourage his son, Jack, to be more open. Jack says that seeing Gus be more comfortable with showing emotion has helped him feel like he can be the same way. He says he sees his dad cry when animals die in cartoons and he knows it isn't a sign of weakness, just of empathy, of caring for things beyond himself.

"A proper conversation," says Gus, "ends with a man hug, not a handshake."

EMIL ZÁTOPEK

(1922–2000)

Emil grew up in a poor family with seven siblings. At the age of fifteen, he left home to work in a shoe factory. One day, his company told him he'd be running in a big race alongside employees from various other factories.

"But I have no interesting in running," Emil told them. "And anyway, I'm terribly unfit."

They made him run anyway and he finished second out of a hundred.

Four years later, Emil was running for Czechoslovakia. In 1948, Emil won the 10,000 meter at the London Olympics. On September 29, 1951, he broke four world records in one race and became the first person to run 20 kilometers in less than an hour.

At the 1952 Helsinki Olympics, Emil won gold in the 5,000 meters and the 10,000 meters. At the last minute, and even though he had absolutely no experience in it, Emil decided to compete in the marathon. He won by more than two minutes.

Despite all of that, his running style was often criticized for being strange and ugly. He made strange facial expressions. One sportswriter wrote that he ran like a man with a scorpion in each shoe.

But Emil didn't mind. He became a legend, but he never forgot what was important: more than anything, Emil loved people and valued friendship over victory. He would study foreign-language dictionaries before international competitions so he could chatter away to other contestants. One night, Emil gave up his bed in the athletes' Olympic Village to a random Australian man with nowhere to sleep. He would help anyone who asked for tips on training and once gave his socks to a competitor who needed them.

In 1966, Emil even gave one of his gold medals to another long-distance runner simply because he felt he deserved one. Emil was loved by everyone, not just for being an astounding athlete, but for being kind, thoughtful, and a joy to be around.

BEN BROOKS

Ben Brooks was born in 1992 and lives in Berlin. He is the author of several books, including *Grow Up* and *Lolito*, which won the Somerset Maugham Award in 2015. He is the author of the international bestsellers *Stories for Boys Who Dare to Be Different* and *Stories for Kids Who Dare to Be Different*.

QUINTON WINTER

Quinton Winter is a British illustrator, artist, and colorist. He has worked for many clients including the *Guardian* newspaper, Walker Books, "Googlebox," *2000AD*, Vertigo Comics, *Mojo*, and the BBC. He is the illustrator of the international bestsellers *Stories for Boys Who Dare to Be Different* and *Stories for Kids Who Dare to Be Different*.

MAKE YOUR OWN GEODESIC DOME

1   Cut out the shape, including flaps

2   Fold along all the blue dotted lines

3   Stick together using the flaps